Caroline Hall

people only
to wound me
that they know so well

but to please me
they have no idea

KEATS

POEMS PUBLISHED IN 1820

EDITED WITH INTRODUCTION AND
NOTES BY

M. ROBERTSON

OXFORD
AT THE CLARENDON PRESS
LONDON : GEOFFREY CUMBERLEGE

PREFACE.

THE text of this edition is a reprint (page for page and line for line) of a copy of the 1820 edition in the British Museum. For convenience of reference line-numbers have been added; but this is the only change, beyond the correction of one or two misprints.

The books to which I am most indebted for the material used in the Introduction and Notes are *The Poems of John Keats* with an Introduction and Notes by E. de Sélincourt, *Life of Keats* (English Men of Letters Series) by Sidney Colvin, and *Letters of John Keats* edited by Sidney Colvin. As a pupil of Dr. de Sélincourt I also owe him special gratitude for his inspiration and direction of my study of Keats, as well as for the constant help which I have received from him in the preparation of this edition.

M. R.

IMPRESSION OF 1952
FIRST EDITION 1909

PRINTED IN GREAT BRITAIN

CONTENTS.

	PAGE
PREFACE	ii
LIFE OF KEATS	v
ADVERTISEMENT . . . . . . ,	2
LAMIA. PART I	3
LAMIA. PART II	27
ISABELLA; OR, THE POT OF BASIL. A STORY FROM BOCCACCIO	47
THE EVE OF ST. AGNES	81
ODE TO A NIGHTINGALE	107
ODE ON A GRECIAN URN	113
ODE TO PSYCHE	117
FANCY	122
ODE ['Bards of Passion and of Mirth'] . .	128
LINES ON THE MERMAID TAVERN . . .	131
ROBIN HOOD. TO A FRIEND	133
TO AUTUMN	137
ODE ON MELANCHOLY	140
HYPERION. BOOK I	145
HYPERION. BOOK II	167
HYPERION. BOOK III	191
NOTE ON ADVERTISEMENT	201
INTRODUCTION TO LAMIA	201
NOTES ON LAMIA	203

a 2

PAGE

INTRODUCTION TO ISABELLA AND THE EVE OF
    ST. AGNES 210

  NOTES ON ISABELLA 215

  NOTES ON THE EVE OF ST. AGNES . . . 224

INTRODUCTION TO THE ODE TO A NIGHTINGALE,
    ODE ON A GRECIAN URN, ODE ON MELAN-
    CHOLY, AND TO AUTUMN 229

  NOTES ON ODE TO A NIGHTINGALE . . . 232

  NOTES ON ODE ON A GRECIAN URN . . . 235

INTRODUCTION TO ODE TO PSYCHE . . . 236

  NOTES ON ODE TO PSYCHE 237

INTRODUCTION TO FANCY 238

  NOTES ON FANCY 238

  NOTES ON ODE ['Bards of Passion and of Mirth'] 239

INTRODUCTION TO LINES ON THE MERMAID TAVERN 239

  NOTES ON LINES ON THE MERMAID TAVERN . 239

INTRODUCTION TO ROBIN HOOD . . . 240

  NOTES ON ROBIN HOOD 241

  NOTES ON 'TO AUTUMN' 242

  NOTES ON ODE ON MELANCHOLY . . . 243

INTRODUCTION TO HYPERION 244

  NOTES ON HYPERION 249

LIFE OF KEATS.

Of all the great poets of the early nineteenth century — Wordsworth, Coleridge, Scott, Byron, Shelley, Keats—John Keats was the last born and the first to die. The length of his life was not one-third that of Wordsworth, who was born twenty-five years before him and outlived him by twenty-nine. Yet before his tragic death at twenty-six Keats had produced a body of poetry of such extraordinary power and promise that the world has sometimes been tempted, in its regret for what he might have done had he lived, to lose sight of the superlative merit of what he actually accomplished.

The three years of his poetic career, during which he published three small volumes of poetry, show a development at the same time rapid and steady, and a gradual but complete abandonment of almost every fault and weakness. It would probably be impossible, in the history of literature, to find such another instance of the 'growth of a poet's mind'.

The last of these three volumes, which is here

reprinted, was published in 1820, when it 'had good success among the literary people and . . . a moderate sale'. It contains the flower of his poetic production and is perhaps, altogether, one of the most marvellous volumes ever issued from the press.

But in spite of the maturity of Keats's work when he was twenty-five, he had been in no sense a precocious child. Born in 1795 in the city of London, the son of a livery-stable keeper, he was brought up amid surroundings and influences by no means calculated to awaken poetic genius.

He was the eldest of five—four boys, one of whom died in infancy, and a girl younger than all; and he and his brothers George and Tom were educated at a private school at Enfield. Here John was at first distinguished more for fighting than for study, whilst his bright, brave, generous nature made him popular with masters and boys.

Soon after he had begun to go to school his father died, and when he was fifteen the children lost their mother too. Keats was passionately devoted to his mother; during her last illness he would sit up all night with her, give her her medicine, and even cook her food himself. At her death he was broken-hearted.

The children were now put under the care of two guardians, one of whom, Mr. Abbey, taking the sole responsibility, immediately removed John from school and apprenticed him for five years to a surgeon at Edmonton.

Whilst thus employed Keats spent all his leisure time in reading, for which he had developed a great enthusiasm during his last two years at school. There he had devoured every book that came in his way, especially rejoicing in stories of the gods and goddesses of ancient Greece. At Edmonton he was able to continue his studies by borrowing books from his friend Charles Cowden Clarke, the son of his schoolmaster, and he often went over to Enfield to change his books and to discuss those which he had been reading. On one of these occasions Cowden Clarke introduced him to Spenser, to whom so many poets have owed their first inspiration that he has been called 'the poets' poet'; and it was then, apparently, that Keats was first prompted to write.

When he was nineteen, a year before his apprenticeship came to an end, he quarrelled with his master, left him, and continued his training in London as a student at St. Thomas's Hospital and Guy's.

Gradually, however, during the months that followed, though he was an industrious and able medical student, Keats came to realize that poetry was his true vocation; and as soon as he was of age, in spite of the opposition of his guardian, he decided to abandon the medical profession and devote his life to literature.

If Mr. Abbey was unsympathetic Keats was not without encouragement from others. His brothers always believed in him whole-heartedly, and his exceptionally lovable nature had won him many friends. Amongst these friends two men older than himself, each famous in his own sphere, had special influence upon him.

One of them, Leigh Hunt, was something of a poet himself and a pleasant prose-writer. His encouragement did much to stimulate Keats's genius, but his direct influence on his poetry was wholly bad. Leigh Hunt's was not a deep nature; his poetry is often trivial and sentimental, and his easy conversational style is intolerable when applied to a great theme. To this man's influence, as well as to the surroundings of his youth, are doubtless due the occasional flaws of taste in Keats's early work.

The other, Haydon, was an artist of mediocre

creative talent but great aims and amazing belief in himself. He had a fine critical faculty which was shown in his appreciation of the Elgin marbles, in opposition to the most respected authorities of his day. Mainly through his insistence they were secured for the nation which thus owes him a boundless debt of gratitude. He helped to guide and direct Keats's taste by his enthusiastic exposition of these masterpieces of Greek sculpture.

In 1817 Keats published his first volume of poems, including 'Sleep and Poetry' and the well-known lines 'I stood tiptoe upon a little hill'. With much that is of the highest poetic value, many memorable lines and touches of his unique insight into nature, the volume yet showed considerable immaturity. It contained indeed, if we except one perfect sonnet, rather a series of experiments than any complete and finished work. There were abundant faults for those who liked to look for them, though there were abundant beauties too; and the critics and the public chose rather to concentrate their attention on the former. The volume was therefore anything but a success; but Keats was not discouraged, for he saw many of his own faults more clearly than did his critics, and felt his power to outgrow them.

Immediately after this Keats went to the Isle of Wight and thence to Margate that he might study and write undisturbed. On May 10th he wrote to Haydon—'I never quite despair, and I read Shakespeare—indeed I shall, I think, never read any other book much'. We have seen Keats influenced by Spenser and by Leigh Hunt: now, though his love for Spenser continued, Shakespeare's had become the dominant influence. Gradually he came too under the influence of Wordsworth's philosophy of poetry and life, and later his reading of Milton affected his style to some extent, but Shakespeare's influence was the widest, deepest and most lasting, though it is the hardest to define. His study of other poets left traces upon his work in turns of phrase or turns of thought: Shakespeare permeated his whole being, and his influence is to be detected not in a resemblance of style, for Shakespeare can have no imitators, but in a broadening view of life, and increased humanity.

No poet could have owed his education more completely to the English poets than did John Keats. His knowledge of Latin was slight—he knew no Greek, and even the classical stories which he loved and constantly used, came to him almost entirely

through the medium of Elizabethan translations and
allusions. In this connexion it is interesting to read
his first fine sonnet, in which he celebrates his introduction to the greatest of Greek poets in the trans-
lation of the rugged and forcible Elizabethan, George
Chapman :—

On first looking into Chapman's Homer.

Much have I travelled in the realms of gold,
And many goodly states and kingdoms seen ;
Round many western islands have I been
Which bards in fealty to Apollo hold.
Oft of one wide expanse had I been told
That deep-brow'd Homer ruled as his demesne ;
Yet did I never breathe its pure serene
Till I heard Chapman speak out loud and bold :
Then felt I like some watcher of the skies
When a new planet swims into his ken ;
Or like stout Cortez when with eagle eyes
He stared at the Pacific—and all his men
Look'd at each other with a wild surmise—
Silent, upon a peak in Darien.

Of the work upon which he was now engaged, the
narrative-poem of *Endymion*, we may give his own

account to his little sister Fanny in a letter dated
September 10th, 1817 :—

'Perhaps you might like to know what I am
writing about. I will tell you. Many years ago
there was a young handsome Shepherd who fed his
flocks on a Mountain's Side called Latmus—he was
a very contemplative sort of a Person and lived
solitary among the trees and Plains little thinking
that such a beautiful Creature as the Moon was
growing mad in Love with him.—However so it
was ; and when he was asleep she used to come
down from heaven and admire him excessively for
a long time ; and at last could not refrain from
carrying him away in her arms to the top of that
high Mountain Latmus while he was a dreaming—
but I dare say you have read this and all the other
beautiful tales which have come down from the
ancient times of that beautiful Greece.'

On his return to London he and his brother Tom,
always delicate and now quite an invalid, took
lodgings at Hampstead. Here Keats remained for
some time, harassed by the illness of his brother
and of several of his friends ; and in June he was
still further depressed by the departure of his brother
George to try his luck in America.

In April, 1818, *Endymion* was finished. Keats was by no means satisfied with it but preferred to publish it as it was, feeling it to be ' as good as I had power to make it by myself '.—' I will write independently ' he says to his publisher—' I have written independently *without judgment*. I may write independently and *with judgment* hereafter. In *Endymion* I leaped headlong into the sea, and thereby have become better acquainted with the soundings, the quicksands, and the rocks, than if I had stayed upon the green shore, and piped a silly pipe, and took tea and comfortable advice.' He published it with a preface modestly explaining to the public his own sense of its imperfection. Nevertheless a storm of abuse broke upon him from the critics who fastened upon all the faults of the poem—the diffuseness of the story, its occasional sentimentality and the sometimes fantastic coinage of words,[1] and ignored the extraordinary beauties of which it is full.

Directly after the publication of *Endymion*, and before the appearance of these reviews, Keats started with a friend, Charles Brown, for a walking tour in

---

[1] Many of the words which the reviewers thought to be coined were good Elizabethan.

Scotland. They first visited the English lakes and
thence walked to Dumfries, where they saw the
house of Burns and his grave. They entered next
the country of Meg Merrilies, and from Kirkcud-
brightshire crossed over to Ireland for a few days.
On their return they went north as far as Argyleshire,
whence they sailed to Staffa and saw Fingal's cave,
which, Keats wrote, 'for solemnity and grandeur
far surpasses the finest Cathedral.' They then crossed
Scotland through Inverness, and Keats returned
home by boat from Cromarty.

His letters home are at first full of interest and
enjoyment, but a 'slight sore throat', contracted
in 'a most wretched walk of thirty-seven miles
across the Isle of Mull', proved very troublesome
and finally cut short his holiday. This was the
beginning of the end. There was consumption in
the family : Tom was dying of it ; and the cold,
wet, and over-exertion of his Scotch tour seem
to have developed the fatal tendency in Keats
himself.

From this time forward he was never well, and no
good was done to either his health or spirits by the
task which now awaited him of tending on his dying
brother. For the last two or three months of 1818,

until Tom's death in December, he scarcely left the bedside, and it was well for him that his friend, Charles Armitage Brown, was at hand to help and comfort him after the long strain. Brown persuaded Keats at once to leave the house, with its sad associations, and to come and live with him.

Before long poetry absorbed Keats again; and the first few months of 1819 were the most fruitful of his life. Besides working at *Hyperion,* which he had begun during Tom's illness, he wrote *The Eve of St. Agnes, The Eve of St. Mark, La Belle Dame Sans Merci,* and nearly all his famous odes.

Troubles however beset him. His friend Haydon was in difficulties and tormenting him, poor as he was, to lend him money; the state of his throat gave serious cause for alarm; and, above all, he was consumed by an unsatisfying passion for the daughter of a neighbour, Mrs. Brawne. She had rented Brown's house whilst they were in Scotland, and had now moved to a street near by. Miss Fanny Brawne returned his love, but she seems never to have understood his nature or his needs. High-spirited and fond of pleasure she did not apparently allow the thought of her invalid lover to interfere much with her enjoyment of life. She would not, however,

abandon her engagement, and she probably gave
him all which it was in her nature to give. Ill-
health made him, on the other hand, morbidly
dissatisfied and suspicious; and, as a result of his
illness and her limitations, his love throughout
brought him restlessness and torment rather than
peace and comfort.

Towards the end of July he went to Shanklin and
there, in collaboration with Brown, wrote a play,
Otho the Great. Brown tells us how they used
to sit, one on either side of a table, he sketching out
the scenes and handing each one, as the outline was
finished, to Keats to write. As Keats never knew
what was coming it was quite impossible that the
characters should be adequately conceived, or that
the drama should be a united whole. Nevertheless
there is much that is beautiful and promising in it.
It should not be forgotten that Keats's 'greatest
ambition' was, in his own words, 'the writing of
a few fine plays'; and, with the increasing humanity
and grasp which his poetry shows, there is no reason
to suppose that, had he lived, he would not have
fulfilled it.

At Shanklin, moreover, he had begun to write
Lamia, and he continued it at Winchester. Here he

stayed until the middle of October, excepting a few days which he spent in London to arrange about the sending of some money to his brother in America. George had been unsuccessful in his commercial enterprises, and Keats, in view of his family's ill-success, determined temporarily to abandon poetry, and by reviewing or journalism to support himself and earn money to help his brother. Then, when he could afford it, he would return to poetry.

Accordingly he came back to London, but his health was breaking down, and with it his resolution. He tried to re-write *Hyperion*, which he felt had been written too much under the influence of Milton and in 'the artist's humour'. The same independence of spirit which he had shown in the publication of *Endymion* urged him now to abandon a work the style of which he did not feel to be absolutely his own. The re-cast he wrote in the form of a vision, calling it *The Fall of Hyperion*, and in so doing he added much to his conception of the meaning of the story. In no poem does he show more of the profoundly philosophic spirit which characterizes many of his letters. But it was too late; his power was failing and, in spite of the beauty and interest of

b

some of his additions, the alterations are mostly for
the worse.

Whilst *The Fall of Hyperion* occupied his evenings
his mornings were spent over a satirical fairy-poem,
The Cap and Bells, in the metre of the *Faerie Queene*.
This metre, however, was ill-suited to the subject;
satire was not natural to him, and the poem has little
intrinsic merit.

Neither this nor the re-cast of *Hyperion* was
finished when, in February, 1820, he had an attack
of illness in which the first definite symptom of
consumption appeared.   Brown tells how he came
home on the evening of Thursday, February 3rd, in
a state of high fever, chilled from having ridden
outside the coach on a bitterly cold day.   'He mildly
and instantly yielded to my request that he should
go to bed . . . On entering the cold sheets, before his
head was on the pillow, he slightly coughed, and
I heard him say—" that is blood from my mouth ".
I went towards him : he was examining a single
drop of blood upon the sheet.   " Bring me the candle,
Brown, and let me see this blood."   After regarding
it steadfastly he looked up in my face with a calmness
of expression that I can never forget, and said,
" I know the colour of that blood ;—it is arterial

blood ; I cannot be deceived in that colour ; that drop of blood is my death warrant ;—I must die." '

He lived for another year, but it was one long dying : he himself called it his ' posthumous life '.

Keats was one of the most charming of letter-writers. He had that rare quality of entering sympathetically into the mind of the friend to whom he was writing, so that his letters reveal to us much of the character of the recipient as well as of the writer. In the long journal-letters which he wrote to his brother and sister-in-law in America he is probably most fully himself, for there he is with the people who knew him best and on whose under-standing and sympathy he could rely. But in none is the beauty of his character more fully revealed than in those to his little sister Fanny, now seventeen years old, and living with their guardian, Mr. Abbey. He had always been very anxious that they should ' become intimately acquainted, in order ', as he says, ' that I may not only, as you grow up, love you as my only Sister, but confide in you as my dearest friend.' In his most harassing times he continued to write to her, directing her reading, sympathizing in her childish troubles, and constantly thinking of little presents to please her. Her health was to him a matter of paramount concern, and in his last letters to her we find him reiterating warnings to take care of herself.—'You must be careful always to wear warm clothing not only in Frost but in a Thaw.'—'Be careful to let no fretting injure your health as I have suffered it—health is the greatest of blessings—with *health* and *hope* we should be content to live, and so you will find as you grow older.' The constant recurrence of this thought becomes, in the light of his own sufferings, almost unbearably pathetic.

During the first months of his illness Keats saw through the press his last volume of poetry, of which this is a reprint. The praise which it received from reviewers and public was in marked contrast to the scornful reception of his earlier works, and would have augured well for the future. But Keats was past caring much for poetic fame. He dragged on through the summer, with rallies and relapses, tormented above all by the thought that death would separate him from the woman he loved. Only Brown, of all his friends, knew what he was suffering, and it seems that he only knew fully after they were parted.

The doctors warned Keats that a winter in England would kill him, so in September, 1820, he left London for Naples, accompanied by a young artist, Joseph Severn, one of his many devoted friends. Shelley, who knew him slightly, invited him to stay at Pisa, but Keats refused. He had never cared for Shelley, though Shelley seems to have liked him, and, in his invalid state, he naturally shrank from being a burden to a mere acquaintance.

It was as they left England, off the coast of Dorsetshire, that Keats wrote his last beautiful sonnet on a blank leaf of his folio copy of Shakespeare, facing *A Lover's Complaint* :—

Bright star! would I were steadfast as thou art—
Not in lone splendour hung aloft the night,
And watching, with eternal lids apart,
Like Nature's patient, sleepless Eremite,
The moving waters at their priest-like task
Of pure ablution round earth's human shores,
Or gazing on the new soft-fallen mask
Of snow upon the mountains and the moors—
No—yet still steadfast, still unchangeable,
Pillow'd upon my fair love's ripening breast,
To feel for ever its soft fall and swell,

> Awake for ever in a sweet unrest,
>
> Still, still to hear her tender taken breath,
>
> And so live ever—or else swoon to death.

The friends reached Rome, and there Keats, after a brief rally, rapidly became worse. Severn nursed him with desperate devotion, and of Keats's sweet considerateness and patience he could never say enough. Indeed such was the force and lovableness of Keats's personality that though Severn lived fifty-eight years longer it was for the rest of his life a chief occupation to write and draw his memories of his friend.

On February 23rd, 1821, came the end for which Keats had begun to long. He died peacefully in Severn's arms. On the 26th he was buried in the beautiful little Protestant cemetery of which Shelley said that it 'made one in love with death to think that one should be buried in so sweet a place'.

Great indignation was felt at the time by those who attributed his death, in part at least, to the cruel treatment which he had received from the critics. Shelley, in *Adonais*, withered them with his scorn, and Byron, in *Don Juan*, had his gibe both at the poet and at his enemies. But we know now how mistaken they were. Keats, in a normal state of mind and body, was never unduly depressed by harsh or unfair criticism. 'Praise or blame,' he wrote, 'has but a momentary effect on the man whose love of beauty in the abstract makes him a severe critic on his own works,' and this attitude he consistently maintained throughout his poetic career. No doubt the sense that his genius was unappreciated added something to the torment of mind which he suffered in Rome, and on his death-bed he asked that on his tombstone should be inscribed the words 'Here lies one whose name was writ in water'. But it was apparently not said in bitterness, and the rest of the inscription [1] expresses rather the natural anger of his friends at the treatment he had received than the mental attitude of the poet himself.

Fully to understand him we must read his poetry with the commentary of his letters which reveal in his character elements of humour, clear-sighted

[1] This Grave contains all that was Mortal of a Young English Poet, who on his Death Bed, in the Bitterness of his Heart at the Malicious Power of his Enemies, desired these Words to be engraven on his Tomb Stone 'Here lies One Whose Name was writ in Water' Feb. 24th 1821.

wisdom, frankness, strength, sympathy and toler-
ance. So doing we shall enter into the mind and
heart of the friend who, speaking for many, described
Keats as one ' whose genius I did not, and do not,
more fully admire than I entirely loved the man '.

LAMIA,

ISABELLA,

THE EVE OF ST. AGNES,

AND

OTHER POEMS.

BY JOHN KEATS,

AUTHOR OF ENDYMION.

LONDON:

PRINTED FOR TAYLOR AND HESSEY,

FLEET-STREET.

1820.

ADVERTISEMENT.

If any apology be thought necessary for the appearance of the unfinished poem of HYPERION, the publishers beg to state that they alone are responsible, as it was printed at their particular request, and contrary to the wish of the author. The poem was intended to have been of equal length with ENDYMION, but the reception given to that work discouraged the author from proceeding.

Fleet-Street, June 26. 1820.

LAMIA.

———

PART I.

UPON a time, before the faery broods
Drove Nymph and Satyr from the prosperous woods,
Before King Oberon's bright diadem,
Sceptre, and mantle, clasp'd with dewy gem,
Frighted away the Dryads and the Fauns
From rushes green, and brakes, and cowslip'd lawns,
The ever-smitten Hermes empty left
His golden throne, bent warm on amorous theft:

classic theme

From high Olympus had he stolen light,
On this side of Jove's clouds, to escape the sight 10
Of his great summoner, and made retreat
Into a forest on the shores of Crete.
For somewhere in that sacred island dwelt
A nymph, to whom all hoofed Satyrs knelt;
At whose white feet the languid Tritons poured
Pearls, while on land they wither'd and adored.
Fast by the springs where she to bathe was wont,
And in those meads where sometime she might haunt,
Were strewn rich gifts, unknown to any Muse,
Though Fancy's casket were unlock'd to choose. 20
Ah, what a world of love was at her feet!
So Hermes thought, and a celestial heat
Burnt from his winged heels to either ear,
That from a whiteness, as the lily clear,
Blush'd into roses 'mid his golden hair,
Fallen in jealous curls about his shoulders bare.

From vale to vale, from wood to wood, he flew,

Breathing upon the flowers his passion new,

And wound with many a river to its head,   29

To find where this sweet nymph prepar'd her secret bed:

In vain; the sweet nymph might nowhere be found,

And so he rested, on the lonely ground,

Pensive, and full of painful jealousies

Of the Wood-Gods, and even the very trees.

There as he stood, he heard a mournful voice,

Such as once heard, in gentle heart, destroys

All pain but pity: thus the lone voice spake:

" When from this wreathed tomb shall I awake!

" When move in a sweet body fit for life,

" And love, and pleasure, and the ruddy strife   40

" Of hearts and lips! Ah, miserable me!"

The God, dove-footed, glided silently

Round bush and tree, soft-brushing, in his speed,

The taller grasses and full-flowering weed,

Until he found a palpitating snake,
Bright, and cirque-couchant in a dusky brake.

                    knotted
  She was a gordian shape of dazzling hue,
Vermilion-spotted, golden, green, and blue ;
Striped like a zebra, freckled like a pard,
Eyed like a peacock, and all crimson barr'd ;   50
And full of silver moons, that, as she breathed,
Dissolv'd, or brighter shone, or interwreathed
Their lustres with the gloomier tapestries—
So rainbow-sided, touch'd with miseries,
She seem'd, at once, some penanced lady elf,
Some demon's mistress, or the demon's self.
Upon her crest she wore a wannish fire
Sprinkled with stars, like Ariadne's tiara
Her head was serpent, but ah, bitter-sweet !   59
She had a woman's mouth with all its pearls complete :
And for her eyes : what could such eyes do there

But weep, and weep, that they were born so fair ?
As Proserpine still weeps for her Sicilian air.
Her throat was serpent, but the words she spake
Came, as through bubbling honey, for Love's sake,
And thus ; while Hermes on his pinions lay,
Like a stoop'd falcon ere he takes his prey.

  " Fair Hermes, crown'd with feathers, fluttering light,
" I had a splendid dream of thee last night :
" I saw thee sitting, on a throne of gold,   10
" Among the Gods, upon Olympus old,
" The only sad one ; for thou didst not hear
" The soft, lute-finger'd Muses chaunting clear,
" Nor even Apollo when he sang alone,
" Deaf to his throbbing throat's long, long melodious
          moan.
" I dreamt I saw thee, robed in purple flakes,
" Break amorous through the clouds, as morning breaks,

" And, swiftly as a bright Phœbean dart,

" Strike for the Cretan isle ; and here thou art !

" Too gentle Hermes, hast thou found the maid ? " 80

Whereat the star of Lethe not delay'd

His rosy eloquence, and thus inquired :

" Thou smooth-lipp'd serpent, surely high inspired !

" Thou beauteous wreath, with melancholy eyes,

" Possess whatever bliss thou canst devise,

" Telling me only where my nymph is fled,—

" Where she doth breathe ! " " Bright planet, thou
          hast said,"

Return'd the snake, " but seal with oaths, fair God ! "

" I swear," said Hermes, " by my serpent rod,

" And by thine eyes, and by thy starry crown ! " 90

Light flew his earnest words, among the blossoms
          blown.

Then thus again the brilliance feminine :

" Too frail of heart ! for this lost nymph of thine,

" Free as the air, invisibly, she strays

" About these thornless wilds ; her pleasant days

" She tastes unseen ; unseen her nimble feet

" Leave traces in the grass and flowers sweet ;

" From weary tendrils, and bow'd branches green,

" She plucks the fruit unseen, she bathes unseen :

" And by my power is her beauty veil'd   100

" To keep it unaffronted, unassail'd

" By the love-glances of unlovely eyes,

" Of Satyrs, Fauns, and blear'd Silenus' sighs.

" Pale grew her immortality, for woe

" Of all these lovers, and she grieved so

" I took compassion on her, bade her steep

" Her hair in weïrd syrops, that would keep

" Her loveliness invisible, yet free

" To wander as she loves, in liberty.

" Thou shalt behold her, Hermes, thou alone,   110

" If thou wilt, as thou swearest, grant my boon ! "

Then, once again, the charmed God began

An oath, and through the serpent's ears it ran

Warm, tremulous, devout, psalterian.

Ravish'd, she lifted her Circean head,

Blush'd a live damask, and swift-lisping said,

" I was a woman, let me have once more

" A woman's shape, and charming as before.

" I love a youth of Corinth—O the bliss!   119

" Give me my woman's form, and place me where he is.

" Stoop, Hermes, let me breathe upon thy brow,

" And thou shalt see thy sweet nymph even now."

The God on half-shut feathers sank serene,

She breath'd upon his eyes, and swift was seen

Of both the guarded nymph near-smiling on the green.

It was no dream; or say a dream it was,

Real are the dreams of Gods, and smoothly pass

Their pleasures in a long immortal dream.

One warm, flush'd moment, hovering, it might seem

Dash'd by the wood-nymph's beauty, so he burn'd ;

Then, lighting on the printless verdure, turn'd 131

To the swoon'd serpent, and with languid arm,

Delicate, put to proof the lythe Caducean charm.

So done, upon the nymph his eyes he bent

Full of adoring tears and blandishment,

And towards her stept : she, like a moon in wane,

Faded before him, cower'd, nor could restrain

Her fearful sobs, self-folding like a flower

That faints into itself at evening hour :

But the God fostering her chilled hand,   140

She felt the warmth, her eyelids open'd bland,

And, like new flowers at morning song of bees,

Bloom'd, and gave up her honey to the lees.

Into the green-recessed woods they flew ;

Nor grew they pale, as mortal lovers do.

   Left to herself, the serpent now began

To change ; her elfin blood in madness ran,

Her mouth foam'd, and the grass, therewith besprent,
Wither'd at dew so sweet and virulent;
Her eyes in torture fix'd, and anguish drear,   150
Hot, glaz'd, and wide, with lid-lashes all sear,
Flash'd phosphor and sharp sparks, without one cooling
  tear.
The colours all inflam'd throughout her train,
She writh'd about, convuls'd with scarlet pain:
A deep volcanian yellow took the place
Of all her milder-mooned body's grace;
And, as the lava ravishes the mead,
Spoilt all her silver mail, and golden brede,
Made gloom of all her frecklings, streaks and bars,
Eclips'd her crescents, and lick'd up her stars: 160
So that, in moments few, she was undrest
Of all her sapphires, greens, and amethyst,
And rubious-argent: of all these bereft,
Nothing but pain and ugliness were left.

Still shone her crown; that vanish'd, also she
Melted and disappear'd as suddenly;
And in the air, her new voice luting soft,
Cried, " Lycius! gentle Lycius!"—Borne aloft
With the bright mists about the mountains hoar
These words dissolv'd : Crete's forests heard no more.

Whither fled Lamia, now a lady bright,   171
A full-born beauty new and exquisite ?
She fled into that valley they pass o'er
Who go to Corinth from Cenchreas' shore;
And rested at the foot of those wild hills,
The rugged founts of the Peræan rills,
And of that other ridge whose barren back
Stretches, with all its mist and cloudy rack,
South-westward to Cleone.   There she stood
About a young bird's flutter from a wood,   180
Fair, on a sloping green of mossy tread,
By a clear pool, wherein she passioned

To see herself escap'd from so sore ills,
While her robes flaunted with the daffodils.

  Ah, happy Lycius !—for she was a maid
More beautiful than ever twisted braid,
Or sigh'd, or blush'd, or on spring-flowered lea
Spread a green kirtle to the minstrelsy :
A virgin purest lipp'd, yet in the lore
Of love deep learned to the red heart's core :   190
Not one hour old, yet of sciential brain
To unperplex bliss from its neighbour pain ;
Define their pettish limits, and estrange
Their points of contact, and swift counterchange ;
Intrigue with the specious chaos, and dispart
Its most ambiguous atoms with sure art ;
As though in Cupid's college she had spent
Sweet days a lovely graduate, still unshent,
And kept his rosy terms in idle languishment.

Why this fair creature chose so fairily   200
By the wayside to linger, we shall see ;
But first 'tis fit to tell how she could muse
And dream, when in the serpent prison-house,
Of all she list, strange or magnificent :
How, ever, where she will'd, her spirit went ;
Whether to faint Elysium, or where
Down through tress-lifting waves the Nereids fair
Wind into Thetis' bower by many a pearly stair ;
Or where God Bacchus drains his cups divine,
Stretch'd out, at ease, beneath a glutinous pine ; 210
Or where in Pluto's gardens palatine
Mulciber's columns gleam in far piazzian line.
And sometimes into cities she would send
Her dream, with feast and rioting to blend ;
And once, while among mortals dreaming thus,
She saw the young Corinthian Lycius
Charioting foremost in the envious race,
Like a young Jove with calm uneager face,

And fell into a swooning love of him.

Now on the moth-time of that evening dim   220

He would return that way, as well she knew,

To Corinth from the shore; for freshly blew

The eastern soft wind, and his galley now

Grated the quaystones with her brazen prow

In port Cenchreas, from Egina isle

Fresh anchor'd; whither he had been awhile

To sacrifice to Jove, whose temple there

Waits with high marble doors for blood and incense rare.

Jove heard his vows, and better'd his desire;

For by some freakful chance he made retire   230

From his companions, and set forth to walk,

Perhaps grown wearied of their Corinth talk:

Over the solitary hills he fared,

Thoughtless at first, but ere eve's star appeared

His phantasy was lost, where reason fades,

In the calm'd twilight of Platonic shades.

Lamia beheld him coming, near, more near—
Close to her passing, in indifference drear,
His silent sandals swept the mossy green ;
So neighbour'd to him, and yet so unseen   240
She stood : he pass'd, shut up in mysteries,
His mind wrapp'd like his mantle, while her eyes
Follow'd his steps, and her neck regal white
Turn'd—syllabling thus, " Ah, Lycius bright,
" And will you leave me on the hills alone ?
" Lycius, look back ! and be some pity shown."
He did ; not with cold wonder fearingly,
But Orpheus-like at an Eurydice ;
For so delicious were the words she sung,
It seem'd he had lov'd them a whole summer long : 250
And soon his eyes had drunk her beauty up,
Leaving no drop in the bewildering cup,
And still the cup was full,—while he, afraid
Lest she should vanish ere his lip had paid

Due adoration, thus began to adore;

Her soft look growing coy, she saw his chain so sure

" Leave thee alone! Look back! Ah, Goddess, see

" Whether my eyes can ever turn from thee!

" For pity do not this sad heart belie—

" Even as thou vanishest so I shall die.   260

" Stay! though a Naiad of the rivers, stay!

" To thy far wishes will thy streams obey:

" Stay! though the greenest woods be thy domain,

" Alone they can drink up the morning rain:

" Though a descended Pleiad, will not one

" Of thine harmonious sisters keep in tune

" Thy spheres, and as thy silver proxy shine?

" So sweetly to these ravish'd ears of mine

" Came thy sweet greeting, that if thou shouldst fade

" Thy memory will waste me to a shade:—   270

" For pity do not melt!"—"If I should stay,"

Said Lamia, " here, upon this floor of clay,

" And pain my steps upon these flowers too rough,

" What canst thou say or do of charm enough

" To dull the nice remembrance of my home ?

" Thou canst not ask me with thee here to roam

" Over these hills and vales, where no joy is,—

" Empty of immortality and bliss !

" Thou art a scholar, Lycius, and must know

" That finer spirits cannot breathe below　　　280

" In human climes, and live : Alas ! poor youth,

" What taste of purer air hast thou to soothe

" My essence ? What serener palaces,

" Where I may all my many senses please,

" And by mysterious sleights a hundred thirsts appease?

" It cannot be—Adieu ! " So said, she rose

Tiptoe with white arms spread. He, sick to lose

The amorous promise of her lone complain,

Swoon'd, murmuring of love, and pale with pain.

c 2

The cruel lady, without any show   290
Of sorrow for her tender favourite's woe,
But rather, if her eyes could brighter be,
With brighter eyes and slow amenity,
Put her new lips to his, and gave afresh
The life she had so tangled in her mesh:
And as he from one trance was wakening
Into another, she began to sing,
Happy in beauty, life, and love, and every thing,
A song of love, too sweet for earthly lyres,
While, like held breath, the stars drew in their pant-
          ing fires.   300
And then she whisper'd in such trembling tone,
As those who, safe together met alone
For the first time through many anguish'd days,
Use other speech than looks; bidding him raise
His drooping head, and clear his soul of doubt,
For that she was a woman, and without

Any more subtle fluid in her veins

Than throbbing blood, and that the self-same pains

Inhabited her frail-strung heart as his.

And next she wonder'd how his eyes could miss 310

Her face so long in Corinth, where, she said,

She dwelt but half retir'd, and there had led

Days happy as the gold coin could invent

Without the aid of love; yet in content

Till she saw him, as once she pass'd him by,

Where 'gainst a column he leant thoughtfully

At Venus' temple porch, 'mid baskets heap'd

Of amorous herbs and flowers, newly reap'd

Late on that eve, as 'twas the night before

The Adonian feast; whereof she saw no more, 320

But wept alone those days, for why should she adore ?

Lycius from death awoke into amaze,

To see her still, and singing so sweet lays ;

Then from amaze into delight he fell

To hear her whisper woman's lore so well;

And every word she spake entic'd him on

To unperplex'd delight and pleasure known.

Let the mad poets say whate'er they please

Of the sweets of Fairies, Peris, Goddesses,

There is not such a treat among them all,   330

Haunters of cavern, lake, and waterfall,

As a real woman, lineal indeed   *direct descendant*

From Pyrrha's pebbles or old Adam's seed.

Thus gentle Lamia judg'd, and judg'd aright,

That Lycius could not love in half a fright,

So threw the goddess off, and won his heart

More pleasantly by playing woman's part,

With no more awe than what her beauty gave,

That, while it smote, still guaranteed to save.

Lycius to all made eloquent reply,   340

Marrying to every word a twinborn sigh;

And last, pointing to Corinth, ask'd her sweet,
If 'twas too far that night for her soft feet.
The way was short, for Lamia's eagerness
Made, by a spell, the triple league decrease
To a few paces ; not at all surmised
By blinded Lycius, so in her comprized.
They pass'd the city gates, he knew not how,
So noiseless, and he never thought to know.

As men talk in a dream, so Corinth all,   350
Throughout her palaces imperial,
And all her populous streets and temples lewd,
Mutter'd, like tempest in the distance brew'd,
To the wide-spreaded night above her towers.
Men, women, rich and poor, in the cool hours,
Shuffled their sandals o'er the pavement white,
Companion'd or alone ; while many a light
Flared, here and there, from wealthy festivals,
And threw their moving shadows on the walls,

Or found them cluster'd in the corniced shade 360
Of some arch'd temple door, or dusky colonnade.

  Muffling his face, of greeting friends in fear,
Her fingers he press'd hard, as one came near
With curl'd gray beard, sharp eyes, and smooth bald
      crown,
Slow-stepp'd, and robed in philosophic gown :
Lycius shrank closer, as they met and past,
Into his mantle, adding wings to haste,
While hurried Lamia trembled : " Ah," said he,
" Why do you shudder, love, so ruefully ?
" Why does your tender palm dissolve in dew ? "—370
" I'm wearied," said fair Lamia : " tell me who
" Is that old man ? I cannot bring to mind
" His features :—Lycius ! wherefore did you blind
" Yourself from his quick eyes ? "   Lycius replied,
" 'Tis Apollonius sage, my trusty guide

" And good instructor ; but to-night he seems
" The ghost of folly haunting my sweet dreams."

  While yet he spake they had arrived before
A pillar'd porch, with lofty portal door,
Where hung a silver lamp, whose phosphor glow 380
Reflected in the slabbed steps below,
Mild as a star in water ; for so new,
And so unsullied was the marble hue,
So through the crystal polish, liquid fine,
Ran the dark veins, that none but feet divine
Could e'er have touch'd there. Sounds Æolian
Breath'd from the hinges, as the ample span
Of the wide doors disclos'd a place unknown
Some time to any, but those two alone,
And a few Persian mutes, who that same year 390
Were seen about the markets : none knew where

They could inhabit; the most curious
Were foil'd, who watch'd to trace them to their house:
And but the flitter-winged verse must tell
For truth's sake, what woe afterwards befel,
'Twould humour many a heart to leave them thus,
Shut from the busy world of more incredulous.

LAMIA.

PART II.

LOVE in a hut, with water and a crust,
Is—Love, forgive us !—cinders, ashes, dust ;
Love in a palace is perhaps at last
More grievous torment than a hermit's fast :—
That is a doubtful tale from faery land,
Hard for the non-elect to understand.
Had Lycius liv'd to hand his story down,
He might have given the moral a fresh frown,
Or clench'd it quite : but too short was their bliss 9
To breed distrust and hate, that make the soft voice hiss

Besides, there, nightly, with terrific glare,
Love, jealous grown of so complete a pair,
Hover'd and buzz'd his wings, with fearful roar,
Above the lintel of their chamber door,
And down the passage cast a glow upon the floor.

    For all this came a ruin : side by side
They were enthroned, in the even tide,
Upon a couch, near to a curtaining
Whose airy texture, from a golden string,
Floated into the room, and let appear   20
Unveil'd the summer heaven, blue and clear,
Betwixt two marble shafts :—there they reposed,
Where use had made it sweet, with eyelids closed,
Saving a tythe which love still open kept,
That they might see each other while they almost slept;
When from the slope side of a suburb hill,
Deafening the swallow's twitter, came a thrill

Of trumpets—Lycius started—the sounds fled,

But left a thought, a buzzing in his head.

For the first time, since first he harbour'd in   30

That purple-lined palace of sweet sin,

His spirit pass'd beyond its golden bourn

Into the noisy world almost forsworn.

The lady, ever watchful, penetrant,

Saw this with pain, so arguing a want

Of something more, more than her empery

Of joys ; and she began to moan and sigh

Because he mused beyond her, knowing well

That but a moment's thought is passion's passing bell.

" Why do you sigh, fair creature ? " whisper'd he : 40

" Why do you think ? " return'd she tenderly :

" You have deserted me ;—where am I now ?

" Not in your heart while care weighs on your brow :

" No, no, you have dismiss'd me ; and I go

" From your breast houseless : ay, it must be so."

He answer'd, bending to her open eyes,

Where he was mirror'd small in paradise,

" My silver planet, both of eve and morn !

" Why will you plead yourself so sad forlorn,

" While I am striving how to fill my heart   50

" With deeper crimson, and a double smart ?

" How to entangle, trammel up and snare

" Your soul in mine, and labyrinth you there

" Like the hid scent in an unbudded rose ?

" Ay, a sweet kiss—you see your mighty woes.

" My thoughts ! shall I unveil them ? Listen then !

" What mortal hath a prize, that other men

" May be confounded and abash'd withal,

" But lets it sometimes pace abroad majestical,

" And triumph, as in thee I should rejoice   60

" Amid the hoarse alarm of Corinth's voice.

" Let my foes choke, and my friends shout afar,

" While through the thronged streets your bridal car

" Wheels round its dazzling spokes."—The lady's cheek
Trembled ; she nothing said, but, pale and meek,
Arose and knelt before him, wept a rain
Of sorrows at his words ; at last with pain
Beseeching him, the while his hand she wrung,
To change his purpose. He thereat was stung,
Perverse, with stronger fancy to reclaim   70
Her wild and timid nature to his aim :
Besides, for all his love, in self despite
Against his better self, he took delight
Luxurious in her sorrows, soft and new.
His passion, cruel grown, took on a hue
Fierce and sanguineous as 'twas possible
In one whose brow had no dark veins to swell.
Fine was the mitigated fury, like
Apollo's presence when in act to strike
The serpent—Ha, the serpent ! certes, she   80
Was none. She burnt, she lov'd the tyranny,

And, all subdued, consented to the hour

When to the bridal he should lead his paramour.

Whispering in midnight silence, said the youth,

" Sure some sweet name thou hast, though, by my truth,

" I have not ask'd it, ever thinking thee

" Not mortal, but of heavenly progeny,

" As still I do. Hast any mortal name,

" Fit appellation for this dazzling frame ?

" Or friends or kinsfolk on the citied earth,   90

" To share our marriage feast and nuptial mirth ? "

" I have no friends," said Lamia, " no, not one ;

" My presence in wide Corinth hardly known :

" My parents' bones are in their dusty urns

" Sepulchred, where no kindled incense burns,

" Seeing all their luckless race are dead, save me,

" And I neglect the holy rite for thee.

" Even as you list invite your many guests ;

" But if, as now it seems, your vision rests

" With any pleasure on me, do not bid   100
" Old Apollonius—from him keep me hid."
Lycius, perplex'd at words so blind and blank,
Made close inquiry; from whose touch she shrank,
Feigning a sleep; and he to the dull shade
Of deep sleep in a moment was betray'd.

   It was the custom then to bring away
The bride from home at blushing shut of day,
Veil'd, in a chariot, heralded along
By strewn flowers, torches, and a marriage song,
With other pageants : but this fair unknown   110
Had not a friend. So being left alone,
(Lycius was gone to summon all his kin)
And knowing surely she could never win
His foolish heart from its mad pompousness,
She set herself, high-thoughted, how to dress

The misery in fit magnificence.

She did so, but 'tis doubtful how and whence

Came, and who were her subtle servitors.

About the halls, and to and from the doors,

There was a noise of wings, till in short space 120

The glowing banquet-room shone with wide-arched

       grace.

A haunting music, sole perhaps and lone

Supportress of the faery-roof, made moan

Throughout, as fearful the whole charm might fade.

Fresh carved cedar, mimicking a glade

Of palm and plantain, met from either side,

High in the midst, in honour of the bride:

Two palms and then two plantains, and so on,

From either side their stems branch'd one to one

All down the aisled place; and beneath all   130

There ran a stream of lamps straight on from wall to

       wall.

So canopied, lay an untasted feast
Teeming with odours. Lamia, regal drest,
Silently paced about, and as she went,
In pale contented sort of discontent,
Mission'd her viewless servants to enrich
The fretted splendour of each nook and niche.
Between the tree-stems, marbled plain at first,
Came jasper pannels ; then, anon, there burst
Forth creeping imagery of slighter trees,   140
And with the larger wove in small intricacies.
Approving all, she faded at self-will,
And shut the chamber up, close, hush'd and still,
Complete and ready for the revels rude,
When dreadful guests would come to spoil her
        solitude.

The day appear'd, and all the gossip rout.
O senseless Lycius ! Madman ! wherefore flout

The silent-blessing fate, warm cloister'd hours,

And show to common eyes these secret bowers ?

The herd approach'd ; each guest, with busy brain,

Arriving at the portal, gaz'd amain,   151

And enter'd marveling : for they knew the street.

Remember'd it from childhood all complete

Without a gap, yet ne'er before had seen

That royal porch, that high-built fair demesne ;

So in they hurried all, maz'd, curious and keen :

Save one, who look'd thereon with eye severe,

And with calm-planted steps walk'd in austere ;

'Twas Apollonius : something too he laugh'd,

As though some knotty problem, that had daft 160

His patient thought, had now begun to thaw,

And solve and melt :—'twas just as he foresaw.

He met within the murmurous vestibule

His young disciple. " 'Tis no common rule,

" Lycius," said he, " for uninvited guest

" To force himself upon you, and infest

" With an unbidden presence the bright throng

" Of younger friends ; yet must I do this wrong,

" And you forgive me." Lycius blush'd, and led

The old man through the inner doors broad-spread ;

With reconciling words and courteous mien　　　171

Turning into sweet milk the sophist's spleen.

Of wealthy lustre was the banquet-room,

Fill'd with pervading brilliance and perfume :

Before each lucid pannel fuming stood

A censer fed with myrrh and spiced wood,

Each by a sacred tripod held aloft,

Whose slender feet wide-swerv'd upon the soft

Wool-woofed carpets : fifty wreaths of smoke

From fifty censers their light voyage took　　　180

To the high roof, still mimick'd as they rose
Along the mirror'd walls by twin-clouds odorous.
Twelve sphered tables, by silk seats insphered,
High as the level of a man's breast rear'd
On libbard's paws, upheld the heavy gold
Of cups and goblets, and the store thrice told
Of Ceres' horn, and, in huge vessels, wine
Come from the gloomy tun with merry shine.
Thus loaded with a feast the tables stood,
Each shrining in the midst the image of a God. 190

When in an antichamber every guest
Had felt the cold full sponge to pleasure press'd,
By minist'ring slaves, upon his hands and feet,
And fragrant oils with ceremony meet
Pour'd on his hair, they all mov'd to the feast
In white robes, and themselves in order placed

Around the silken couches, wondering
Whence all this mighty cost and blaze of wealth could
　　　spring.

　Soft went the music the soft air along,
While fluent Greek a vowel'd undersong　　　200
Kept up among the guests, discoursing low
At first, for scarcely was the wine at flow;
But when the happy vintage touch'd their brains,
Louder they talk, and louder come the strains
Of powerful instruments :—the gorgeous dyes,
The space, the splendour of the draperies,
The roof of awful richness, nectarous cheer,
Beautiful slaves, and Lamia's self, appear,
Now, when the wine has done its rosy deed,
And every soul from human trammels freed,　　　210
No more so strange; for merry wine, sweet wine,
Will make Elysian shades not too fair, too divine.

Soon was God Bacchus at meridian height;
Flush'd were their cheeks, and bright eyes double
    bright:
Garlands of every green, and every scent
From vales deflower'd, or forest-trees branch-rent,
In baskets of bright osier'd gold were brought
High as the handles heap'd, to suit the thought
Of every guest; that each, as he did please,
Might fancy-fit his brows, silk-pillow'd at his ease. 220

    What wreath for Lamia? What for Lycius?
What for the sage, old Apollonius?
Upon her aching forehead be there hung
The leaves of willow and of adder's tongue;
And for the youth, quick, let us strip for him
The thyrsus, that his watching eyes may swim
Into forgetfulness; and, for the sage,
Let spear-grass and the spiteful thistle wage

rod used by Bacchus followers

he's about to be spiteful & ruin everything

War on his temples. Do not all charms fly
At the mere touch of cold philosophy ?　　　　230
There was an awful rainbow once in heaven :
We know her woof, her texture ; she is given
In the dull catalogue of common things.
Philosophy will clip an Angel's wings,
Conquer all mysteries by rule and line,
Empty the haunted air, and gnomed mine—
Unweave a rainbow, as it erewhile made
The tender-person'd Lamia melt into a shade.

By her glad Lycius sitting, in chief place,
Scarce saw in all the room another face,　　　　240
Till, checking his love trance, a cup he took
Full brimm'd, and opposite sent forth a look
'Cross the broad table, to beseech a glance
From his old teacher's wrinkled countenance,

And pledge him. The bald-head philosopher
Had fix'd his eye, without a twinkle or stir
Full on the alarmed beauty of the bride,
Brow-beating her fair form, and troubling her sweet
      pride.

Lycius then press'd her hand, with devout touch,
As pale it lay upon the rosy couch :   250
'Twas icy, and the cold ran through his veins ;
Then sudden it grew hot, and all the pains
Of an unnatural heat shot to his heart.
"Lamia, what means this ? Wherefore dost thou start ?
"Know'st thou that man ?" Poor Lamia answer'd not.
He gaz'd into her eyes, and not a jot
Own'd they the lovelorn piteous appeal :
More, more he gaz'd : his human senses reel :
Some hungry spell that loveliness absorbs ;
There was no recognition in those orbs.   260

" Lamia ! " he cried—and no soft-toned reply.

The many heard, and the loud revelry

Grew hush ; the stately music no more breathes ;

The myrtle sicken'd in a thousand wreaths.

By faint degrees, voice, lute, and pleasure ceased ;

A deadly silence step by step increased,

Until it seem'd a horrid presence there,

And not a man but felt the terror in his hair.

" Lamia ! " he shriek'd ; and nothing but the shriek

With its sad echo did the silence break.   270

" Begone, foul dream ! " he cried, gazing again

In the bride's face, where now no azure vein

Wander'd on fair-spaced temples ; no soft bloom

Misted the cheek ; no passion to illume

The deep-recessed vision :—all was blight ;

Lamia, no longer fair, there sat a deadly white.

" Shut, shut those juggling eyes, thou ruthless man !

" Turn them aside, wretch ! or the righteous ban

" Of all the Gods, whose dreadful images

" Here represent their shadowy presences,   280

" May pierce them on the sudden with the thorn

" Of painful blindness ; leaving thee forlorn,

" In trembling dotage to the feeblest fright

" Of conscience, for their long offended might,

" For all thine impious proud-heart sophistries,

" Unlawful magic, and enticing lies.

" Corinthians ! look upon that gray-beard wretch !

" Mark how, possess'd, his lashless eyelids stretch

" Around his demon eyes ! Corinthians, see !

" My sweet bride withers at their potency."   290

" Fool ! " said the sophist, in an under-tone

Gruff with contempt ; which a death-nighing moan

From Lycius answer'd, as heart-struck and lost,

He sank supine beside the aching ghost.

" Fool ! Fool ! " repeated he, while his eyes still

Relented not, nor mov'd ; " from every ill

" Of life have I preserv'd thee to this day,

" And shall I see thee made a serpent's prey ? "

Then Lamia breath'd death breath ; the sophist's eye,

Like a sharp spear, went through her utterly, 300

Keen, cruel, perceant, stinging : she, as well

As her weak hand could any meaning tell,

Motion'd him to be silent ; vainly so,

He look'd and look'd again a level—No !

" A Serpent ! " echoed he ; no sooner said,

Than with a frightful scream she vanished :

And Lycius' arms were empty of delight,

As were his limbs of life, from that same night.

On the high couch he lay !—his friends came round—

Supported him—no pulse, or breath they found, 310

And, in its marriage robe, the heavy body wound.*

* " Philostratus, in his fourth book *de Vita Apollonii*, hath a
memorable instance in this kind, which I may not omit, of one
Menippus Lycius, a young man twenty-five years of age, that
going betwixt Cenchreas and Corinth, met such a phantasm in the

habit of a fair gentlewoman, which taking him by the hand, carried him home to her house, in the suburbs of Corinth, and told him she was a Phœnician by birth, and if he would tarry with her, he should hear her sing and play, and drink such wine as never any drank, and no man should molest him; but she, being fair and lovely, would live and die with him, that was fair and lovely to behold. The young man, a philosopher, otherwise staid and discreet, able to moderate his passions, though not this of love, tarried with her a while to his great content, and at last married her, to whose wedding, amongst other guests, came Apollonius; who, by some probable conjectures, found her out to be a serpent, a lamia; and that all her furniture was, like Tantalus' gold, described by Homer, no substance but mere illusions. When she saw herself descried, she wept, and desired Apollonius to be silent, but he would not be moved, and thereupon she, plate, house, and all that was in it, vanished in an instant: many thousands took notice of this fact, for it was done in the midst of Greece."

Burton's 'Anatomy of Melancholy.' *Part 3. Sect. 2.*
Memb. 1. *Subs.* 1.

ISABELLA:

OR,

THE POT OF BASIL.

A STORY FROM BOCCACCIO.

ISABELLA:

OR,

THE POT OF BASIL.

—

I.

FAIR Isabel, poor simple Isabel!
  Lorenzo, a young palmer in Love's eye!
They could not in the self-same mansion dwell
  Without some stir of heart, some malady;
They could not sit at meals but feel how well
  It soothed each to be the other by;
They could not, sure, beneath the same roof sleep
But to each other dream, and nightly weep.

II.

With every morn their love grew tenderer,

 With every eve deeper and tenderer still; 10

He might not in house. field, or garden stir,

 But her full shape would all his seeing fill;

And his continual voice was pleasanter

 To her, than noise of trees or hidden rill;

Her lute-string gave an echo of his name,

She spoilt her half-done broidery with the same.

III.

He knew whose gentle hand was at the latch,

 Before the door had given her to his eyes;

And from her chamber-window he would catch

 Her beauty farther than the falcon spies; 20

And constant as her vespers would he watch,

 Because her face was turn'd to the same skies;

And with sick longing all the night outwear,

To hear her morning-step upon the stair.

IV.

A whole long month of May in this sad plight
  Made their cheeks paler by the break of June:
" To-morrow will I bow to my delight,
  " To-morrow will I ask my lady's boon."—
" O may I never see another night,
  " Lorenzo, if thy lips breathe not love's tune."—30
So spake they to their pillows; but, alas,
Honeyless days and days did he let pass;

V.

Until sweet Isabella's untouch'd cheek
  Fell sick within the rose's just domain,
Fell thin as a young mother's, who doth seek
  By every lull to cool her infant's pain:
" How ill she is," said he, " I may not speak,
  " And yet I will, and tell my love all plain:
" If looks speak love-laws, I will drink her tears,
" And at the least 'twill startle off her cares." 40

E 2

VI.

So said he one fair morning, and all day
 His heart beat awfully against his side;
And to his heart he inwardly did pray
 For power to speak; but still the ruddy tide
Stifled his voice, and puls'd resolve away—
 Fever'd his high conceit of such a bride,
Yet brought him to the meekness of a child:
Alas! when passion is both meek and wild!

VII.

So once more he had wak'd and anguished
 A dreary night of love and misery,
If Isabel's quick eye had not been wed
 To every symbol on his forehead high;
She saw it waxing very pale and dead,
 And straight all flush'd; so, lisped tenderly
"Lorenzo!"—here she ceas'd her timid quest,
But in her tone and look he read the rest.

VIII.

" O Isabella, I can half perceive

  " That I may speak my grief into thine ear ;

" If thou didst ever any thing believe,

  " Believe how I love thee, believe how near   60

" My soul is to its doom : I would not grieve

  " Thy hand by unwelcome pressing, would not fear

" Thine eyes by gazing ; but I cannot live

" Another night, and not my passion shrive.

IX.

" Love ! thou art leading me from wintry cold,

  " Lady ! thou leadest me to summer clime,

" And I must taste the blossoms that unfold

  " In its ripe warmth this gracious morning time."

So said, his erewhile timid lips grew bold,

  And poesied with hers in dewy rhyme :   70

Great bliss was with them, and great happiness

Grew, like a lusty flower in June's caress.

X.

Parting they seem'd to tread upon the air,

   Twin roses by the zephyr blown apart

Only to meet again more close, and share

   The inward fragrance of each other's heart.

She, to her chamber gone, a ditty fair

   Sang, of delicious love and honey'd dart;

He with light steps went up a western hill,

And bade the sun farewell, and joy'd his fill.   80

XI.

All close they met again, before the dusk

   Had taken from the stars its pleasant veil,

All close they met, all eves, before the dusk

   Had taken from the stars its pleasant veil,

Close in a bower of hyacinth and musk,

   Unknown of any, free from whispering tale.

Ah! better had it been for ever so,

Than idle ears should pleasure in their woe.

XII.

Were they unhappy then ?—It cannot be—

    Too many tears for lovers have been shed,   90

Too many sighs give we to them in fee,

    Too much of pity after they are dead,

Too many doleful stories do we see,

    Whose matter in bright gold were best be read ;

Except in such a page where Theseus' spouse

Over the pathless waves towards him bows.

XIII.

But, for the general award of love,

    The little sweet doth kill much bitterness ;

Though Dido silent is in under-grove,

    And Isabella's was a great distress,   100

Though young Lorenzo in warm Indian clove

    Was not embalm'd, this truth is not the less:

Even bees, the little almsmen of spring-bowers,

Know there is richest juice in poison-flowers.

XIV.

With her two brothers this fair lady dwelt,
   Enriched from ancestral merchandize,
And for them many a weary hand did swelt
   In torched mines and noisy factories,
And many once proud-quiver'd loins did melt
   In blood from stinging whip ;—with hollow eyes 110
Many all day in dazzling river stood,
To take the rich-ored driftings of the flood.

XV.

For them the Ceylon diver held his breath,
   And went all naked to the hungry shark ;
For them his ears gush'd blood ; for them in death
   The seal on the cold ice with piteous bark
Lay full of darts ; for them alone did seethe
   A thousand men in troubles wide and dark :
Half-ignorant, they turn'd an easy wheel,
That set sharp racks at work, to pinch and peel. 120

XVI.

Why were they proud ? Because their marble founts
  Gush'd with more pride than do a wretch's tears ?—
Why were they proud ? Because fair orange-mounts
  Were of more soft ascent than lazar stairs ?—
Why were they proud ? Because red-lin'd accounts
  Were richer than the songs of Grecian years ?—
Why were they proud ? again we ask aloud,
Why in the name of Glory were they proud ?

XVII.

Yet were these Florentines as self-retired
  In hungry pride and gainful cowardice,   130
As two close Hebrews in that land inspired,
  Paled in and vineyarded from beggar-spies
The hawks of ship-mast forests—the untired
  And pannier'd mules for ducats and old lies—
Quick cat's-paws on the generous stray-away,—
Great wits in Spanish, Tuscan, and Malay.

XVIII.

How was it these same ledger-men could spy
  Fair Isabella in her downy nest?
How could they find out in Lorenzo's eye
  A straying from his toil? Hot Egypt's pest 140
Into their vision covetous and sly!
  How could these money-bags see east and west?—
Yet so they did—and every dealer fair
Must see behind, as doth the hunted hare.

XIX.

O eloquent and famed Boccaccio!
  Of thee we now should ask forgiving boon,
And of thy spicy myrtles as they blow,
  And of thy roses amorous of the moon,
And of thy lilies, that do paler grow
  Now they can no more hear thy ghittern's tune, 150
For venturing syllables that ill beseem
The quiet glooms of such a piteous theme.

XX.

Grant thou a pardon here, and then the tale

    Shall move on soberly, as it is meet;

There is no other crime, no mad assail

    To make old prose in modern rhyme more sweet:

But it is done—succeed the verse or fail—

    To honour thee, and thy gone spirit greet;

To stead thee as a verse in English tongue,

An echo of thee in the north-wind sung.   160

XXI.

These brethren having found by many signs

    What love Lorenzo for their sister had,

And how she lov'd him too, each unconfines

    His bitter thoughts to other, well nigh mad

That he, the servant of their trade designs,

    Should in their sister's love be blithe and glad,

When 'twas their plan to coax her by degrees

To some high noble and his olive-trees.

XXII.

And many a jealous conference had they,

　And many times they bit their lips alone,　　170

Before they fix'd upon a surest way

　To make the youngster for his crime atone;

And at the last, these men of cruel clay

　Cut Mercy with a sharp knife to the bone;

For they resolved in some forest dim

To kill Lorenzo, and there bury him.

XXIII.

So on a pleasant morning, as he leant

　Into the sun-rise, o'er the balustrade

Of the garden-terrace, towards him they bent

　Their footing through the dews; and to him said, 180

" You seem there in the quiet of content,

　" Lorenzo, and we are most loth to invade

" Calm speculation; but if you are wise,

" Bestride your steed while cold is in the skies.

XXIV.

" To-day we purpose, ay, this hour we mount
  " To spur three leagues towards the Apennine ;
" Come down, we pray thee, ere the hot sun count
  " His dewy rosary on the eglantine."
Lorenzo, courteously as he was wont,
  Bow'd a fair greeting to these serpents' whine ; 190
And went in haste, to get in readiness,
With belt, and spur, and bracing huntsman's dress.

XXV.

And as he to the court-yard pass'd along,
  Each third step did he pause, and listen'd oft
If he could hear his lady's matin-song,
  Or the light whisper of her footstep soft ;
And as he thus over his passion hung,
  He heard a laugh full musical aloft ;
When, looking up, he saw her features bright
Smile through an in-door lattice, all delight.   200

XXVI.

"Love, Isabel!" said he, "I was in pain

  "Lest I should miss to bid thee a good morrow

"Ah! what if I should lose thee, when so fain

  "I am to stifle all the heavy sorrow

"Of a poor three hours' absence? but we'll gain

  "Out of the amorous dark what day doth borrow.

"Good bye! I'll soon be back."—"Good bye!" said she:—

And as he went she chanted merrily.

XXVII.

So the two brothers and their murder'd man

  Rode past fair Florence, to where Arno's stream 210

Gurgles through straiten'd banks, and still doth fan

  Itself with dancing bulrush, and the bream

Keeps head against the freshets. Sick and wan

  The brothers' faces in the ford did seem,

Lorenzo's flush with love.—They pass'd the water

Into a forest quiet for the slaughter.

XXVIII.

There was Lorenzo slain and buried in,
  There in that forest did his great love cease;
Ah! when a soul doth thus its freedom win,
  It aches in loneliness—is ill at peace   220
As the break-covert blood-hounds of such sin:
  They dipp'd their swords in the water, and did tease
Their horses homeward, with convulsed spur,
Each richer by his being a murderer.

XXIX.

They told their sister how, with sudden speed,
  Lorenzo had ta'en ship for foreign lands,
Because of some great urgency and need
  In their affairs, requiring trusty hands.
Poor Girl! put on thy stifling widow's weed,
  And 'scape at once from Hope's accursed bands; 230
To-day thou wilt not see him, nor to-morrow,
And the next day will be a day of sorrow.

XXX.

She weeps alone for pleasures not to be;
　　Sorely she wept until the night came on,
And then, instead of love, O misery!
　　She brooded o'er the luxury alone:
His image in the dusk she seem'd to see,
　　And to the silence made a gentle moan,
Spreading her perfect arms upon the air,　　239
And on her couch low murmuring "Where? O where?"

XXXI.

But Selfishness, Love's cousin, held not long
　　Its fiery vigil in her single breast;
She fretted for the golden hour, and hung
　　Upon the time with feverish unrest—
Not long—for soon into her heart a throng
　　Of higher occupants, a richer zest,
Came tragic; passion not to be subdued,
And sorrow for her love in travels rude.

XXXII.

In the mid days of autumn, on their eves

   The breath of Winter comes from far away, 250

And the sick west continually bereaves

   Of some gold tinge, and plays a roundelay

Of death among the bushes and the leaves

   To make all bare before he dares to stray

From his north cavern. So sweet Isabel

By gradual decay from beauty fell,

XXXIII.

Because Lorenzo came not. Oftentimes

   She ask'd her brothers, with an eye all pale,

Striving to be itself, what dungeon climes

   Could keep him off so long? They spake a tale 260

Time after time, to quiet her. Their crimes

   Came on them, like a smoke from Hinnom's vale;

And every night in dreams they groan'd aloud,

To see their sister in her snowy shroud.

XXXIV.

would have

And she had died in drowsy ignorance,

But for a thing more deadly dark than all;
It came like a fierce potion, drunk by chance,

Which saves a sick man from the feather'd pall
For some few gasping moments; like a lance,

Waking an Indian from his cloudy hall   270
With cruel pierce, and bringing him again
Sense of the gnawing fire at heart and brain.

XXXV.

It was a vision.—In the drowsy gloom,

The dull of midnight, at her couch's foot
Lorenzo stood, and wept: the forest tomb

Had marr'd his glossy hair which once could shoot
Lustre into the sun, and put cold doom

Upon his lips, and taken the soft lute
From his lorn voice, and past his loamed ears
Had made a miry channel for his tears.   280

XXXVI.

Strange sound it was, when the pale shadow spake ;
  For there was striving, in its piteous tongue,
To speak as when on earth it was awake,
  And Isabella on its music hung :
Languor there was in it, and tremulous shake,
  As in a palsied Druid's harp unstrung ;
And through it moan'd a ghostly under-song,
Like hoarse night-gusts sepulchral briars among.

XXXVII.

Its eyes, though wild, were still all dewy bright
  With love, and kept all phantom fear aloof   290
From the poor girl by magic of their light,
  The while it did unthread the horrid woof
Of the late darken'd time,—the murderous spite
  Of pride and avarice,—the dark pine roof
In the forest,—and the sodden turfed dell,
Where, without any word, from stabs he fell.

XXXVIII.

Saying moreover, " Isabel, my sweet!

    " Red whortle-berries droop above my head,

" And a large flint-stone weighs upon my feet;

    " Around me beeches and high chestnuts shed 300

" Their leaves and prickly nuts; a sheep-fold bleat

    " Comes from beyond the river to my bed:

" Go, shed one tear upon my heather-bloom,

" And it shall comfort me within the tomb.

XXXIX.

" I am a shadow now, alas! alas!

    " Upon the skirts of human-nature dwelling

" Alone: I chant alone the holy mass,

    " While little sounds of life are round me knelling,

" And glossy bees at noon do fieldward pass.

    " And many a chapel bell the hour is telling, 310

" Paining me through: those sounds grow strange to me,

" And thou art distant in Humanity.

XL.

" I know what was, I feel full well what is,

" And I should rage, if spirits could go mad;

" Though I forget the taste of earthly bliss,

" That paleness warms my grave, as though I had

" A Seraph chosen from the bright abyss

" To be my spouse : thy paleness makes me glad;

" Thy beauty grows upon me, and I feel

" A greater love through all my essence steal." 320

XLI.

The Spirit mourn'd " Adieu ! "—dissolv'd, and left

The atom darkness in a slow turmoil;

As when of healthful midnight sleep bereft,

Thinking on rugged hours and fruitless toil,

We put our eyes into a pillowy cleft,

And see the spangly gloom froth up and boil :

It made sad Isabella's eyelids ache,

And in the dawn she started up awake;

XLII.

"Ha! ha!" said she, "I knew not this hard life,
  "I thought the worst was simple misery;   330
"·I thought some Fate with pleasure or with strife
  "Portion'd us—happy days, or else to die;
"But there is crime—a brother's bloody knife!
  "Sweet Spirit, thou hast school'd my infancy:
"I'll visit thee for this, and kiss thine eyes,
"And greet thee morn and even in the skies."

XLIII.

When the full morning came, she had devised
  How she might secret to the forest hie;
How she might find the clay, so dearly prized,
  And sing to it one latest lullaby;   340
How her short absence might be unsurmised,
  While she the inmost of the dream would try.
Resolv'd, she took with her an aged nurse,
And went into that dismal forest-hearse.

XLIV.

See, as they creep along the river side,

How she doth whisper to that aged Dame,

And, after looking round the champaign wide,

Shows her a knife.—" What feverous hectic flame

" Burns in thee, child ?—What good can thee betide,

" That thou should'st smile again ? "—The evening
came,   350

And they had found Lorenzo's earthy bed ;

The flint was there, the berries at his head.

XLV.

Who hath not loiter'd in a green church-yard,

And let his spirit, like a demon-mole,

Work through the clayey soil and gravel hard,

To see scull, coffin'd bones, and funeral stole ;

Pitying each form that hungry Death hath marr'd,

And filling it once more with human soul ?

Ah ! this is holiday to what was felt

When Isabella by Lorenzo knelt.   360

XLVI.

She gaz'd into the fresh-thrown mould, as though
   One glance did fully all its secrets tell;
Clearly she saw, as other eyes would know
   Pale limbs at bottom of a crystal well;
Upon the murderous spot she seem'd to grow,
   Like to a native lily of the dell:
Then with her knife, all sudden, she began
To dig more fervently than misers can.

XLVII.

Soon she turn'd up a soiled glove, whereon
   Her silk had play'd in purple phantasies,   370
She kiss'd it with a lip more chill than stone,
   And put it in her bosom, where it dries
And freezes utterly unto the bone
   Those dainties made to still an infant's cries:
Then 'gan she work again; nor stay'd her care,
But to throw back at times her veiling hair.

XLVIII.

That old nurse stood beside her wondering,

  Until her heart felt pity to the core

At sight of such a dismal labouring,

  And so she kneeled, with her locks all hoar, 380

And put her lean hands to the horrid thing:

  Three hours they labour'd at this travail sore;

At last they felt the kernel of the grave,

And Isabella did not stamp and rave.

XLIX.

Ah! wherefore all this wormy circumstance?

  Why linger at the yawning tomb so long?

O for the gentleness of old Romance,

  The simple plaining of a minstrel's song!

Fair reader, at the old tale take a glance,

  For here, in truth, it doth not well belong   390

To speak:—O turn thee to the very tale,

And taste the music of that vision pale.

L.

With duller steel than the Perséan sword
  They cut away no formless monster's head,
But one, whose gentleness did well accord
  With death, as life.   The ancient harps have said,
Love never dies, but lives, immortal Lord :
  If Love impersonate was ever dead,
Pale Isabella kiss'd it, and low moan'd.
'Twas love ; cold,—dead indeed, but not dethroned. 400

LI.

In anxious secrecy they took it home,
  And then the prize was all for Isabel :
She calm'd its wild hair with a golden comb,
  And all around each eye's sepulchral cell
Pointed each fringed lash ; the smeared loam
  With tears, as chilly as a dripping well,
She drench'd away :—and still she comb'd, and kept
Sighing all day—and still she kiss'd, and wept.

LII.

Then in a silken scarf,—sweet with the dews
  Of precious flowers pluck'd in Araby,   410
And divine liquids come with odorous ooze
  Through the cold serpent-pipe refreshfully,—
She wrapp'd it up; and for its tomb did choose
  A garden-pot, wherein she laid it by,
And cover'd it with mould, and o'er it set
Sweet Basil, which her tears kept ever wet.

LIII.

And she forgot the stars, the moon, and sun,
  And she forgot the blue above the trees,
And she forgot the dells where waters run,
  And she forgot the chilly autumn breeze;   420
She had no knowledge when the day was done,
  And the new morn she saw not: but in peace
Hung over her sweet Basil evermore,
And moisten'd it with tears unto the core.

LIV.

And so she ever fed it with thin tears,

    Whence thick, and green, and beautiful it grew,

So that it smelt more balmy than its peers

    Of Basil-tufts in Florence ; for it drew

Nurture besides, and life, from human fears,

    From the fast mouldering head there shut from view:

So that the jewel, safely casketed,   431

Came forth, and in perfumed leafits spread.

LV.

O Melancholy, linger here awhile !

    O Music, Music, breathe despondingly !

O Echo, Echo, from some sombre isle,

    Unknown, Lethean, sigh to us—O sigh !

Spirits in grief, lift up your heads, and smile ;

    Lift up your heads, sweet Spirits, heavily,

And make a pale light in your cypress glooms,

Tinting with silver wan your marble tombs.   440

LVI.

Moan hither, all ye syllables of woe,
From the deep throat of sad Melpomene.
Through bronzed lyre in tragic order go,
And touch the strings into a mystery;
Sound mournfully upon the winds and low;
For simple Isabel is soon to be
Among the dead: She withers, like a palm
Cut by an Indian for its juicy balm.

LVII.

O leave the palm to wither by itself;
Let not quick Winter chill its dying hour!— 450
It may not be—those Baälites of pelf,
Her brethren, noted the continual shower
From her dead eyes; and many a curious elf,
Among her kindred, wonder'd that such dower
Of youth and beauty should be thrown aside
By one mark'd out to be a Noble's bride.

LVIII.

And, furthermore, her brethren wonder'd much
  Why she sat drooping by the Basil green,
And why it flourish'd, as by magic touch;
  Greatly they wonder'd what the thing might mean:
They could not surely give belief, that such   461
  A very nothing would have power to wean
Her from her own fair youth, and pleasures gay,
And even remembrance of her love's delay.

LIX.

Therefore they watch'd a time when they might sift
  This hidden whim; and long they watch'd in vain;
For seldom did she go to chapel-shrift,
  And seldom felt she any hunger-pain;
And when she left, she hurried back, as swift
  As bird on wing to breast its eggs again;   470
And, patient as a hen-bird, sat her there
Beside her Basil, weeping through her hair.

LX.

Yet they contriv'd to steal the Basil-pot,
    And to examine it in secret place :
The thing was vile with green and livid spot,
    And yet they knew it was Lorenzo's face :
The guerdon of their murder they had got,
    And so left Florence in a moment's space,
Never to turn again.—Away they went,
With blood upon their heads, to banishment.   480

LXI.

O Melancholy, turn thine eyes away !
    O Music, Music, breathe despondingly !
O Echo, Echo, on some other day,
    From isles Lethean, sigh to us—O sigh !
Spirits of grief, sing not your " Well-a-way ! "
    For Isabel, sweet Isabel, will die ;
Will die a death too lone and incomplete,
Now they have ta'en away her Basil sweet.

LXII.

Piteous she look'd on dead and senseless things,

    Asking for her lost Basil amorously;   490

And with melodious chuckle in the strings

    Of her lorn voice, she oftentimes would cry

After the Pilgrim in his wanderings,

    To ask him where her Basil was; and why

Twas hid from her: "For cruel 'tis," said she,

"To steal my Basil-pot away from me."

LXIII.

And so she pined, and so she died forlorn,

    Imploring for her Basil to the last.

No heart was there in Florence but did mourn

    In pity of her love, so overcast.   500

And a sad ditty of this story born

    From mouth to mouth through all the country pass'd:

Still is the burthen sung—"O cruelty,

"To steal my Basil-pot away from me!"

THE

EVE OF ST. AGNES.

EVE OF ST. AGNES

I.

St. Agnes' Eve—Ah, bitter chill it was!
The owl, for all his feathers, was a-cold;
The hare limp'd trembling through the frozen grass,
And silent was the flock in woolly fold:
Numb were the Beadsman's fingers, while he told
His rosary, and while his frosted breath,
Like pious incense from a censer old,
Seem'd taking flight for heaven, without a death,
Past the sweet Virgin's picture, while his prayer he saith.

II.

His prayer he saith, this patient, holy man;   10
Then takes his lamp, and riseth from his knees,
And back returneth, meagre, barefoot, wan,
Along the chapel aisle by slow degrees:
The sculptur'd dead, on each side, seem to freeze,
Emprison'd in black, purgatorial rails:
Knights, ladies, praying in dumb orat'ries,
He passeth by; and his weak spirit fails
To think how they may ache in icy hoods and mails.

III.

Northward he turneth through a little door,
And scarce three steps, ere Music's golden tongue   20
Flatter'd to tears this aged man and poor;
But no—already had his deathbell rung;
The joys of all his life were said and sung:
His was harsh penance on St. Agnes' Eve:
Another way he went, and soon among
Rough ashes sat he for his soul's reprieve,
And all night kept awake, for sinners' sake to grieve.

IV.

That ancient Beadsman heard the prelude soft;
And so it chanc'd, for many a door was wide,
From hurry to and fro. Soon, up aloft,   30
The silver, snarling trumpets 'gan to chide:
The level chambers, ready with their pride,
Were glowing to receive a thousand guests:
The carved angels, ever eager-eyed,
Star'd, where upon their heads the cornice rests,
With hair blown back, and wings put cross-wise on their
        breasts.

V.

At length burst in the argent revelry,
With plume, tiara, and all rich array,
Numerous as shadows haunting fairily
The brain, new stuff'd, in youth, with triumphs gay 40
Of old romance. These let us wish away,
And turn, sole-thoughted, to one Lady there,
Whose heart had brooded, all that wintry day,
On love, and wing'd St. Agnes' saintly care,
As she had heard old dames full many times declare.

VI.

They told her how, upon St. Agnes' Eve,
Young virgins might have visions of delight,
And soft adorings from their loves receive
Upon the honey'd middle of the night,
If ceremonies due they did aright;   50
As, supperless to bed they must retire,
And couch supine their beauties, lily white;
Nor look behind, nor sideways, but require
Of Heaven with upward eyes for all that they desire.

VII.

Full of this whim was thoughtful Madeline:
The music, yearning like a God in pain,
She scarcely heard: her maiden eyes divine,
Fix'd on the floor, saw many a sweeping train
Pass by—she heeded not at all: in vain
Came many a tiptoe, amorous cavalier,   60
And back retir'd; not cool'd by high disdain,
But she saw not: her heart was otherwhere:
She sigh'd for Agnes' dreams, the sweetest of the year.

VIII.

She danc'd along with vague, regardless eyes,
  Anxious her lips, her breathing quick and short :
The hallow'd hour was near at hand : she sighs
  Amid the timbrels, and the throng'd resort
Of whisperers in anger, or in sport ;
  'Mid looks of love, defiance, hate, and scorn,
Hoodwink'd with faery fancy ; all amort,   70
  Save to St. Agnes and her lambs unshorn,
And all the bliss to be before to-morrow morn.

IX.

So, purposing each moment to retire,
  She linger'd still. Meantime, across the moors,
Had come young Porphyro, with heart on fire
  For Madeline. Beside the portal doors,
Buttress'd from moonlight, stands he, and implores
  All saints to give him sight of Madeline,
But for one moment in the tedious hours,
  That he might gaze and worship all unseen ;   80
Perchance speak, kneel, touch, kiss—in sooth such things
        have been.

X.

He ventures in : let no buzz'd whisper tell :
All eyes be muffled, or a hundred swords
Will storm his heart, Love's fev'rous citadel :
For him, those chambers held barbarian hordes,
Hyena foemen, and hot-blooded lords,
Whose very dogs would execrations howl
Against his lineage : not one breast affords
Him any mercy, in that mansion foul,
Save one old beldame, weak in body and in soul. 90

XI.

Ah, happy chance ! the aged creature came,
Shuffling along with ivory-headed wand,
To where he stood, hid from the torch's flame,
Behind a broad hall-pillar, far beyond
The sound of merriment and chorus bland :
He startled her ; but soon she knew his face,
And grasp'd his fingers in her palsied hand,
Saying, "Mercy, Porphyro ! hie thee from this place ;
" They are all here to-night, the whole blood-thirsty race !

XII.

"Get hence! get hence! there's dwarfish Hildebrand;
"He had a fever late, and in the fit   101
"He cursed thee and thine, both house and land:
"Then there's that old Lord Maurice, not a whit
"More tame for his gray hairs—Alas me! flit!
"Flit like a ghost away."—"Ah, Gossip dear,
"We're safe enough; here in this arm-chair sit,
"And tell me how"—"Good Saints! not here, not here;
"Follow me, child, or else these stones will be thy bier."

XIII.

He follow'd through a lowly arched way,
Brushing the cobwebs with his lofty plume,   110
And as she mutter'd "Well-a—well-a-day!"
He found him in a little moonlight room,
Pale, lattic'd, chill, and silent as a tomb.
"Now tell me where is Madeline," said he,
"O tell me, Angela, by the holy loom
"Which none but secret sisterhood may see,
"When they St. Agnes' wool are weaving piously."

XIV.

" St. Agnes ! Ah ! it is St. Agnes' Eve—
" Yet men will murder upon holy days :
" Thou must hold water in a witch's sieve,   120
" And be liege-lord of all the Elves and Fays,
" To venture so : it fills me with amaze
" To see thee, Porphyro !—St. Agnes' Eve !
" God's help ! my lady fair the conjuror plays
" This very night : good angels her deceive !
" But let me laugh awhile, I've mickle time to grieve."

XV.

Feebly she laugheth in the languid moon,
While Porphyro upon her face doth look,
Like puzzled urchin on an aged crone
Who keepeth clos'd a wond'rous riddle-book,   130
As spectacled she sits in chimney nook.
But soon his eyes grew brilliant, when she told
His lady's purpose ; and he scarce could brook
Tears, at the thought of those enchantments cold,
And Madeline asleep in lap of legends old.

XVI.

Sudden a thought came like a full-blown rose,

Flushing his brow, and in his pained heart

Made purple riot: then doth he propose

A stratagem, that makes the beldame start:

" A cruel man and impious thou art :   140

" Sweet lady, let her pray, and sleep, and dream

" Alone with her good angels, far apart

" From wicked men like thee. Go, go !—I deem

"Thou canst not surely be the same that thou didst seem."

XVII.

" I will not harm her, by all saints I swear,"

Quoth Porphyro : " O may I ne'er find grace

" When my weak voice shall whisper its last prayer,

" If one of her soft ringlets I displace,

" Or look with ruffian passion in her face :

" Good Angela, believe me by these tears ;   150

" Or I will, even in a moment's space,

" Awake, with horrid shout, my foemen's ears,

" And beard them, though they be more fang'd than

wolves and bears."

XVIII.

" Ah ! why wilt thou affright a feeble soul ?

" A poor, weak, palsy-stricken, churchyard thing,

" Whose passing-bell may ere the midnight toll ;

" Whose prayers for thee, each morn and evening,

"Were never miss'd."—Thus plaining, doth she bring

A gentler speech from burning Porphyro ;

So woful, and of such deep sorrowing,   160

That Angela gives promise she will do

Whatever he shall wish, betide her weal or woe.

XIX.

Which was, to lead him, in close secrecy,

Even to Madeline's chamber, and there hide

Him in a closet, of such privacy

That he might see her beauty unespied,

And win perhaps that night a peerless bride,

While legion'd fairies pac'd the coverlet,

And pale enchantment held her sleepy-eyed.

Never on such a night have lovers met,   170

Since Merlin paid his Demon all the monstrous debt.

XX.

" It shall be as thou wishest," said the Dame :
" All cates and dainties shall be stored there
" Quickly on this feast-night : by the tambour frame
" Her own lute thou wilt see : no time to spare,
" For I am slow and feeble, and scarce dare
" On such a catering trust my dizzy head.
" Wait here, my child, with patience ; kneel in prayer
" The while : Ah ! thou must needs the lady wed,
" Or may I never leave my grave among the dead." 180

XXI.

So saying, she hobbled off with busy fear.
The lover's endless minutes slowly pass'd ;
The dame return'd, and whisper'd in his ear
To follow her ; with aged eyes aghast
From fright of dim espial. Safe at last,
Through many a dusky gallery, they gain
The maiden's chamber, silken, hush'd, and chaste ;
Where Porphyro took covert, pleas'd amain.
His poor guide hurried back with agues in her brain.

XXII.

Her falt'ring hand upon the balustrade,   190
Old Angela was feeling for the stair,
When Madeline, St. Agnes' charmed maid,
Rose, like a mission'd spirit, unaware :
With silver taper's light, and pious care,
She turn'd, and down the aged gossip led
To a safe level matting. Now prepare,
Young Porphyro, for gazing on that bed ;
She comes, she comes again, like ring-dove fray'd and fled.

XXIII.

Out went the taper as she hurried in ;
Its little smoke, in pallid moonshine, died :   200
She clos'd the door, she panted, all akin
To spirits of the air, and visions wide :
No uttered syllable, or, woe betide !
But to her heart, her heart was voluble,
Paining with eloquence her balmy side ;
As though a tongueless nightingale should swell
Her throat in vain, and die, heart-stifled, in her dell.

XXIV.

A casement high and triple-arch'd there was,
All garlanded with carven imag'ries
Of fruits, and flowers, and bunches of knot-grass, 210
And diamonded with panes of quaint device,
Innumerable of stains and splendid dyes,
As are the tiger-moth's deep-damask'd wings;
And in the midst, 'mong thousand heraldries,
And twilight saints, and dim emblazonings,
A shielded scutcheon blush'd with blood of queens and
      kings.

XXV.

Full on this casement shone the wintry moon,
And threw warm gules on Madeline's fair breast,
As down she knelt for heaven's grace and boon;
Rose-bloom fell on her hands, together prest, 220
And on her silver cross soft amethyst,
And on her hair a glory, like a saint:
She seem'd a splendid angel, newly drest,
Save wings, for heaven:—Porphyro grew faint:
She knelt, so pure a thing, so free from mortal taint.

XXVI.

Anon his heart revives : her vespers done,
Of all its wreathed pearls her hair she frees ;
Unclasps her warmed jewels one by one ;
Loosens her fragrant boddice ; by degrees
Her rich attire creeps rustling to her knees : 230
Half-hidden, like a mermaid in sea-weed,
Pensive awhile she dreams awake, and sees,
In fancy, fair St. Agnes in her bed,
But dares not look behind, or all the charm is fled.

XXVII.

Soon, trembling in her soft and chilly nest,
In sort of wakeful swoon, perplex'd she lay,
Until the poppied warmth of sleep oppress'd
Her soothed limbs, and soul fatigued away ;
Flown, like a thought, until the morrow-day ;
Blissfully haven'd both from joy and pain ; 240
Clasp'd like a missal where swart Paynims pray ;
Blinded alike from sunshine and from rain,
As though a rose should shut, and be a bud again.

XXVIII.

Stol'n to this paradise, and so entranced,
Porphyro gazed upon her empty dress,
And listen'd to her breathing, if it chanced
To wake into a slumberous tenderness ;
Which when he heard, that minute did he bless,
And breath'd himself : then from the closet crept,
Noiseless as fear in a wide wilderness,   250
And over the hush'd carpet, silent, stept,
And 'tween the curtains peep'd, where, lo !—how fast
    she slept.

XXIX.

Then by the bed-side, where the faded moon
Made a dim, silver twilight, soft he set
A table, and, half anguish'd, threw thereon
A cloth of woven crimson, gold, and jet :—
O for some drowsy Morphean amulet !
The boisterous, midnight, festive clarion,
The kettle-drum, and far-heard clarionet,
Affray his ears, though but in dying tone :— 260
The hall door shuts again, and all the noise is gone.

XXX.

And still she slept an azure-lidded sleep,
In blanched linen, smooth, and lavender'd,
While he from forth the closet brought a heap
Of candied apple, quince, and plum, and gourd;
With jellies soother than the creamy curd,
And lucent syrops, tinct with cinnamon;
Manna and dates, in argosy transferr'd
From Fez; and spiced dainties, every one,
From silken Samarcand to cedar'd Lebanon.   270

XXXI.

These delicates he heap'd with glowing hand
On golden dishes and in baskets bright
Of wreathed silver: sumptuous they stand
In the retired quiet of the night,
Filling the chilly room with perfume light.—
" And now, my love, my seraph fair, awake!
" Thou art my heaven, and I thine eremite:
" Open thine eyes, for meek St. Agnes' sake,
" Or I shall drowse beside thee, so my soul doth ache."

XXXII.

Thus whispering, his warm, unnerved arm   280
Sank in her pillow. Shaded was her dream
By the dusk curtains :—'twas a midnight charm
Impossible to melt as iced stream :
The lustrous salvers in the moonlight gleam ;
Broad golden fringe upon the carpet lies :
It seem'd he never, never could redeem
From such a stedfast spell his lady's eyes ;
So mus'd awhile, entoil'd in woofed phantasies.

XXXIII.

Awakening up, he took her hollow lute,—
Tumultuous,—and, in chords that tenderest be, 290
He play'd an ancient ditty, long since mute,
In Provence call'd, " La belle dame sans mercy : "
Close to her ear touching the melody ;—
Wherewith disturb'd, she utter'd a soft moan :
He ceased—she panted quick—and suddenly
Her blue affrayed eyes wide open shone :
Upon his knees he sank, pale as smooth-sculptured stone.

H 2

XXXIV.

Her eyes were open, but she still beheld,
Now wide awake, the vision of her sleep:
There was a painful change, that nigh expell'd 30ι
The blisses of her dream so pure and deep
At which fair Madeline began to weep,
And moan forth witless words with many a sigh;
While still her gaze on Porphyro would keep;
Who knelt, with joined hands and piteous eye,
Fearing to move or speak, she look'd so dreamingly.

XXXV.

" Ah, Porphyro ! " said she, " but even now
" Thy voice was at sweet tremble in mine ear,
" Made tuneable with every sweetest vow ;   309
" And those sad eyes were spiritual and clear :
" How chang'd thou art! how pallid, chill, and drear!
" Give me that voice again, my Porphyro,
" Those looks immortal, those complainings dear !
" Oh leave me not in this eternal woe,
" For if thou diest, my Love, I know not where to go."

XXXVI.

Beyond a mortal man impassion'd far
At these voluptuous accents, he arose,
Ethereal, flush'd, and like a throbbing star
Seen mid the sapphire heaven's deep repose;
Into her dream he melted, as the rose   320
Blendeth its odour with the violet,—
Solution sweet: meantime the frost-wind blows
Like Love's alarum pattering the sharp sleet
Against the window-panes; St. Agnes' moon hath set.

XXXVII.

'Tis dark: quick pattereth the flaw-blown sleet:
" This is no dream, my bride, my Madeline ! "
'Tis dark: the iced gusts still rave and beat:
" No dream, alas ! alas ! and woe is mine !
" Porphyro will leave me here to fade and pine.—
" Cruel ! what traitor could thee hither bring ? 330
" I curse not, for my heart is lost in thine,
" Though thou forsakest a deceived thing ;—
" A dove forlorn and lost with sick unpruned wing."

XXXVIII.

"My Madeline! sweet dreamer! lovely bride!
"Say, may I be for aye thy vassal blest?
"Thy beauty's shield, heart-shap'd and vermeil dyed?
"Ah, silver shrine, here will I take my rest
"After so many hours of toil and quest,
"A famish'd pilgrim,—saved by miracle.
"Though I have found, I will not rob thy nest 340
"Saving of thy sweet self; if thou think'st well
"To trust, fair Madeline, to no rude infidel."

XXXIX.

"Hark! 'tis an elfin-storm from faery land,
"Of haggard seeming, but a boon indeed:
"Arise—arise! the morning is at hand;—
"The bloated wassaillers will never heed:—
"Let us away, my love, with happy speed;
"There are no ears to hear, or eyes to see,—
"Drown'd all in Rhenish and the sleepy mead:
"Awake! arise! my love, and fearless be,   350
"For o'er the southern moors I have a home for thee."

XL.

She hurried at his words, beset with fears,
For there were sleeping dragons all around,
At glaring watch, perhaps, with ready spears—
Down the wide stairs a darkling way they found.—
In all the house was heard no human sound.
A chain-droop'd lamp was flickering by each door ;
The arras, rich with horseman, hawk, and hound,
Flutter'd in the besieging wind's uproar ;
And the long carpets rose along the gusty floor. 360

XLI.

They glide, like phantoms, into the wide hall ;
Like phantoms, to the iron porch, they glide ;
Where lay the Porter, in uneasy sprawl,
With a huge empty flaggon by his side :
The wakeful bloodhound rose, and shook his hide,
But his sagacious eye an inmate owns :
By one, and one, the bolts full easy slide :—
The chains lie silent on the footworn stones ;—
The key turns, and the door upon its hinges groans.

XLII.

And they are gone : ay, ages long ago   370
These lovers fled away into the storm.
That night the Baron dreamt of many a woe,
And all his warrior-guests, with shade and form
Of witch, and demon, and large coffin-worm,
Were long be-nightmar'd. Angela the old
Died palsy-twitch'd, with meagre face deform ;
The Beadsman, after thousand aves told,
For aye unsought for slept among his ashes cold.

like the end of a fairy tale.
Romeo & Juliet theme with
a happy ending.

POEMS.

POEMS.

ODE TO A NIGHTINGALE.

1.

mood set

My heart aches, and a drowsy numbness pains
  My sense, as though of hemlock I had drunk,
Or emptied some dull opiate to the drains
  One minute past, and Lethe-wards had sunk:
'Tis not through envy of thy happy lot,
  But being too happy in thine happiness,—
    That thou, light-winged Dryad of the trees,
      In some melodious plot
Of beechen green, and shadows numberless,
  Singest of summer in full-throated ease.   10

melancholy

melancholy feeling melody is beautiful but seems to savour of sadness (joy & pain together)

2.

O, for a draught of vintage! that hath been
   Cool'd a long age in the deep-delved earth,
Tasting of Flora and the country green,
   Dance, and Provençal song, and sunburnt mirth!
O for a beaker full of the warm South,
   Full of the true, the blushful Hippocrene,
     With beaded bubbles winking at the brim,
       And purple-stained mouth;
That I might drink, and leave the world unseen,
   And with thee fade away into the forest dim: 20

3.

Fade far away, dissolve, and quite forget
   What thou among the leaves hast never known,
The weariness, the fever, and the fret
   Here, where men sit and hear each other groan;
Where palsy shakes a few, sad, last gray hairs,

Where youth grows pale, and spectre-thin, and dies;

   Where but to think is to be full of sorrow

      And leaden-eyed despairs,

Where Beauty cannot keep her lustrous eyes,

   Or new Love pine at them beyond to-morrow. 30

4.

Away! away! for I will fly to thee,

  Not chariroted by Bacchus and his pards,

But on the viewless wings of Poesy,

  Though the dull brain perplexes and retards:

Already with thee! tender is the night,

  And haply the Queen-Moon is on her throne,

    Cluster'd around by all her starry Fays;

      But here there is no light,

  Save what from heaven is with the breezes blown

    Through verdurous glooms and winding mossy

  ways.   40

5.

I cannot see what flowers are at my feet,
  Nor what soft incense hangs upon the boughs,
But, in embalmed darkness, guess each sweet
  Wherewith the seasonable month endows
The grass, the thicket, and the fruit-tree wild;
  White hawthorn, and the pastoral eglantine;
    Fast fading violets cover'd up in leaves;
      And mid-May's eldest child,
  The coming musk-rose, full of dewy wine,
    The murmurous haunt of flies on summer eves. 50

6.

Darkling I listen; and, for many a time
  I have been half in love with easeful Death,
Call'd him soft names in many a mused rhyme,
  To take into the air my quiet breath;
Now more than ever seems it rich to die,

To cease upon the midnight with no pain,
   While thou art pouring forth thy soul abroad
      In such an ecstasy!
Still wouldst thou sing, and I have ears in vain—
   To thy high requiem become a sod.   60

7.

Thou wast not born for death, immortal Bird!
  No hungry generations tread thee down;
The voice I hear this passing night was heard
  In ancient days by emperor and clown:
Perhaps the self-same song that found a path
  Through the sad heart of Ruth, when, sick for home,
    She stood in tears amid the alien corn;
      The same that oft-times hath
Charm'd magic casements, opening on the foam
  Of perilous seas, in faery lands forlorn.   70

8.

Forlorn! the very word is like a bell
   To toll me back from thee to my sole self!
Adieu! the fancy cannot cheat so well
   As she is fam'd to do, deceiving elf.
Adieu! adieu! thy plaintive anthem fades
   Past the near meadows, over the still stream,
      Up the hill-side; and now 'tis buried deep
         In the next valley-glades:
Was it a vision, or a waking dream?
   Fled is that music:—Do I wake or sleep?   80

ODE ON A GRECIAN URN.

1.

THOU still unravish'd bride of quietness,
  Thou foster-child of silence and slow time,
Sylvan historian, who canst thus express
  A flowery tale more sweetly than our rhyme:
What leaf-fring'd legend haunts about thy shape
  Of deities or mortals, or of both,
    In Tempe or the dales of Arcady?
  What men or gods are these? What maidens loth?
What mad pursuit? What struggle to escape?
    What pipes and timbrels? What wild ecstasy? 10

1082.2   I

2.

Heard melodies are sweet, but those unheard

   Are sweeter ; therefore, ye soft pipes, play on ;

Not to the sensual ear, but, more endear'd,

   Pipe to the spirit ditties of no tone :

Fair youth, beneath the trees, thou canst not leave

   Thy song, nor ever can those trees be bare ;

    Bold Lover, never, never canst thou kiss,

Though winning near the goal—yet, do not grieve ;

   She cannot fade, though thou hast not thy bliss,

    For ever wilt thou love, and she be fair !   20

3.

Ah, happy, happy boughs ! that cannot shed

   Your leaves, nor ever bid the Spring adieu ;

And, happy melodist, unwearied,

   For ever piping songs for ever new ;

More happy love! more happy, happy love!
  For ever warm and still to be enjoy'd,
    For ever panting, and for ever young;
All breathing human passion far above,
  That leaves a heart high-sorrowful and cloy'd,
    A burning forehead, and a parching tongue. 30

4.

Who are these coming to the sacrifice?
  To what green altar, O mysterious priest,
Lead'st thou that heifer lowing at the skies,
  And all her silken flanks with garlands drest?
What little town by river or sea shore,
  Or mountain-built with peaceful citadel,
    Is emptied of this folk, this pious morn?
And, little town, thy streets for evermore
  Will silent be; and not a soul to tell
    Why thou art desolate, can e'er return.

5.

O Attic shape! Fair attitude! with brede
  Of marble men and maidens overwrought,
With forest branches and the trodden weed;
  Thou, silent form, dost tease us out of thought
As doth eternity: Cold Pastoral!
  When old age shall this generation waste,
    Thou shalt remain, in midst of other woe
Than ours, a friend to man, to whom thou say'st,
  "Beauty is truth, truth beauty,"—that is all
    Ye know on earth, and all ye need to know. 50

ODE TO PSYCHE.

O Goddess! hear these tuneless numbers, wrung
  By sweet enforcement and remembrance dear,
And pardon that thy secrets should be sung
  Even into thine own soft-conched ear:
Surely I dreamt to-day, or did I see
  The winged Psyche with awaken'd eyes?
I wander'd in a forest thoughtlessly,
  And, on the sudden, fainting with surprise,
Saw two fair creatures, couched side by side
  In deepest grass, beneath the whisp'ring roof 10
  Of leaves and trembled blossoms, where there ran
    A brooklet, scarce espied:

Mid hush'd, cool-rooted flowers, fragrant-eyed,
   Blue, silver-white, and budded Tyrian,
They lay calm-breathing on the bedded grass;
   Their arms embraced, and their pinions too;
   Their lips touch'd not, but had not bade adieu,
As if disjoined by soft-handed slumber,
And ready still past kisses to outnumber
   At tender eye-dawn of aurorean love: 20
      The winged boy I knew;
   But who wast thou, O happy, happy dove?
      His Psyche true!

O latest born and loveliest vision far
   Of all Olympus' faded hierarchy!
Fairer than Phœbe's sapphire-region'd star,
   Or Vesper, amorous glow-worm of the sky;
Fairer than these, though temple thou hast none,
     Nor altar heap'd with flowers;

Nor virgin-choir to make delicious moan   30
    Upon the midnight hours;
No voice, no lute, no pipe, no incense sweet
  From chain-swung censer teeming;
No shrine, no grove, no oracle, no heat
  Of pale-mouth'd prophet dreaming.

O brightest! though too late for antique vows,
  Too, too late for the fond believing lyre,
When holy were the haunted forest boughs,
  Holy the air, the water, and the fire;
Yet even in these days so far retir'd   40
  From happy pieties, thy lucent fans,
  Fluttering among the faint Olympians,
I see, and sing, by my own eyes inspired.
So let me be thy choir, and make a moan
    Upon the midnight hours;

Thy voice, thy lute, thy pipe, thy incense sweet
  From swinged censer teeming;
Thy shrine, thy grove, thy oracle, thy heat
  Of pale-mouth'd prophet dreaming.

Yes, I will be thy priest, and build a fane   50
  In some untrodden region of my mind,
Where branched thoughts, new grown with pleasant
        pain,
  Instead of pines shall murmur in the wind:
Far, far around shall those dark-cluster'd trees
  Fledge the wild-ridged mountains steep by steep;
And there by zephyrs, streams, and birds, and bees,
  The moss-lain Dryads shall be lull'd to sleep;
And in the midst of this wide quietness
A rosy sanctuary will I dress
With the wreath'd trellis of a working brain,   60
  With buds, and bells, and stars without a name,

With all the gardener Fancy e'er could feign,
  Who breeding flowers, will never breed the same:
And there shall be for thee all soft delight
  That shadowy thought can win,
A bright torch, and a casement ope at night,
  To let the warm Love in !

FANCY.

EVER let the Fancy roam,
Pleasure never is at home :
At a touch sweet Pleasure melteth,
Like to bubbles when rain pelteth ;
Then let winged Fancy wander
Through the thought still spread beyond her :
Open wide the mind's cage-door,
She'll dart forth, and cloudward soar.
O sweet Fancy ! let her loose ;
Summer's joys are spoilt by use,   10
And the enjoying of the Spring
Fades as does its blossoming ;
Autumn's red-lipp'd fruitage too,
Blushing through the mist and dew

Cloys with tasting: What do then?
Sit thee by the ingle, when
The sear faggot blazes bright,
Spirit of a winter's night;
When the soundless earth is muffled,
And the caked snow is shuffled   20
From the ploughboy's heavy shoon;
When the Night doth meet the Noon
In a dark conspiracy
To banish Even from her sky.
Sit thee there, and send abroad,
With a mind self-overaw'd,
Fancy, high-commission'd :—send her!
She has vassals to attend her :
She will bring, in spite of frost,
Beauties that the earth hath lost;   30
She will bring thee, all together,
All delights of summer weather;

All the buds and bells of May,

From dewy sward or thorny spray

All the heaped Autumn's wealth,

With a still, mysterious stealth:

She will mix these pleasures up

Like three fit wines in a cup,

And thou shalt quaff it :—thou shalt hear

Distant harvest-carols clear ;   40

Rustle of the reaped corn ;

Sweet birds antheming the morn :

And, in the same moment—hark !

'Tis the early April lark,

Or the rooks, with busy caw,

Foraging for sticks and straw.

Thou shalt, at one glance, behold

The daisy and the marigold ;

White-plum'd lilies, and the first

Hedge-grown primrose that hath burst ;   50

Shaded hyacinth, alway
Sapphire queen of the mid-May;
And every leaf, and every flower
Pearled with the self-same shower.
Thou shalt see the field-mouse peep
Meagre from its celled sleep;
And the snake all winter-thin
Cast on sunny bank its skin;
Freckled nest-eggs thou shalt see
Hatching in the hawthorn-tree,   60
When the hen-bird's wing doth rest
Quiet on her mossy nest;
Then the hurry and alarm
When the bee-hive casts its swarm;
Acorns ripe down-pattering,
While the autumn breezes sing.

Oh, sweet Fancy! let her loose;
Every thing is spoilt by use:
Where's the cheek that doth not fade,
Too much gaz'd at? Where's the maid   70
Whose lip mature is ever new?
Where's the eye, however blue,
Doth not weary? Where's the face
One would meet in every place?
Where's the voice, however soft,
One would hear so very oft?
At a touch sweet Pleasure melteth
Like to bubbles when rain pelteth.
Let, then, winged Fancy find
Thee a mistress to thy mind: 80
Dulcet-eyed as Ceres' daughter,
Ere the God of Torment taught her
How to frown and how to chide;
With a waist and with a side

White as Hebe's, when her zone
Slipt its golden clasp, and down
Fell her kirtle to her feet,
While she held the goblet sweet,
And Jove grew languid.—Break the mesh
Of the Fancy's silken leash;   90
Quickly break her prison-string
And such joys as these she'll bring.—
Let the winged Fancy roam,
Pleasure never is at home.

ODE.

BARDS of Passion and of Mirth,
Ye have left your souls on earth!
Have ye souls in heaven too,
Double-lived in regions new?
Yes, and those of heaven commune
With the spheres of sun and moon;
With the noise of fountains wond'rous,
And the parle of voices thund'rous;
With the whisper of heaven's trees
And one another, in soft ease   10
Seated on Elysian lawns
Brows'd by none but Dian's fawns
Underneath large blue-bells tented.
Where the daisies are rose-scented,

And the rose herself has got
Perfume which on earth is not;
Where the nightingale doth sing
Not a senseless, tranced thing.
But divine melodious truth;
Philosophic numbers smooth;   20
Tales and golden histories
Of heaven and its mysteries.

   Thus ye live on high, and then
On the earth ye live again;
And the souls ye left behind you
Teach us, here, the way to find you,
Where your other souls are joying,
Never slumber'd, never cloying.
Here, your earth-born souls still speak
To mortals, of their little week;   30

Of their sorrows and delights;
Of their passions and their spites;
Of their glory and their shame;
What doth strengthen and what maim.
Thus ye teach us, every day,
Wisdom, though fled far away.

Bards of Passion and of Mirth,
Ye have left your souls on earth!
Ye have souls in heaven too,
Double-lived in regions new!   40

LINES

ON

THE MERMAID TAVERN.

SOULS of Poets dead and gone,
What Elysium have ye known,
Happy field or mossy cavern,
Choicer than the Mermaid Tavern ?
Have ye tippled drink more fine
Than mine host's Canary wine ?
Or are fruits of Paradise
Sweeter than those dainty pies
Of venison ? O generous food !
Drest as though bold Robin Hood   10
Would, with his maid Marian,
Sup and bowse from horn and can.

K 2

I have heard that on a day
Mine host's sign-board flew away,
Nobody knew whither, till
An astrologer's old quill
To a sheepskin gave the story,
Said he saw you in your glory,
Underneath a new old-sign
Sipping beverage divine,   20
And pledging with contented smack
The Mermaid in the Zodiac.

Souls of Poets dead and gone,
What Elysium have ye known,
Happy field or mossy cavern,
Choicer than the Mermaid Tavern ?

ROBIN HOOD.

TO A FRIEND.

No! those days are gone away,
And their hours are old and gray,
And their minutes buried all
Under the down-trodden pall
Of the leaves of many years:
Many times have winter's shears,
Frozen North, and chilling East,
Sounded tempests to the feast
Of the forest's whispering fleeces,
Since men knew nor rent nor leases.   10

  No, the bugle sounds no more,
And the twanging bow no more;

Silent is the ivory shrill
Past the heath and up the hill;
There is no mid-forest laugh,
Where lone Echo gives the half
To some wight, amaz'd to hear
Jesting, deep in forest drear.

On the fairest time of June
You may go, with sun or moon,   20
Or the seven stars to light you,
Or the polar ray to right you;
But you never may behold
Little John, or Robin bold;
Never one, of all the clan,
Thrumming on an empty can
Some old hunting ditty, while
He doth his green way beguile
To fair hostess Merriment,
Down beside the pasture Trent;   30

For he left the merry tale
Messenger for spicy ale.

Gone, the merry morris din;
Gone, the song of Gamelyn;
Gone, the tough-belted outlaw
Idling in the " grenè shawe ; "
All are gone away and past !
And if Robin should be cast
Sudden from his turfed grave,
And if Marian should have 40
Once again her forest days,
She would weep, and he would craze :
He would swear, for all his oaks,
Fall'n beneath the dockyard strokes,
Have rotted on the briny seas ;
She would weep that her wild bees
Sang not to her—strange ! that honey
Can't be got without hard money !

So it is : yet let us sing,

Honour to the old bow-string !   50

Honour to the bugle-horn !

Honour to the woods unshorn !

Honour to the Lincoln green !

Honour to the archer keen !

Honour to tight little John,

And the horse he rode upon !

Honour to bold Robin Hood,

Sleeping in the underwood !

Honour to maid Marian,

And to all the Sherwood-clan !   60

Though their days have hurried by

Let us two a burden try.

TO AUTUMN.

1.

Season of mists and mellow fruitfulness,
  Close bosom-friend of the maturing sun;
Conspiring with him how to load and bless
  With fruit the vines that round the thatch-eves run;
To bend with apples the moss'd cottage-trees,
  And fill all fruit with ripeness to the core;
    To swell the gourd, and plump the hazel shells
With a sweet kernel; to set budding more,
  And still more, later flowers for the bees,
  Until they think warm days will never cease,   10
    For Summer has o'er-brimm'd their clammy cells.

2.

Who hath not seen thee oft amid thy store?
  Sometimes whoever seeks abroad may find
Thee sitting careless on a granary floor,
  Thy hair soft-lifted by the winnowing wind;
Or on a half-reap'd furrow sound asleep,
  Drows'd with the fume of poppies, while thy hook
    Spares the next swath and all its twined flowers:
And sometimes like a gleaner thou dost keep
  Steady thy laden head across a brook;   20
  Or by a cyder-press, with patient look,
    Thou watchest the last oozings hours by hours.

3.

Where are the songs of Spring? Ay, where are they?
  Think not of them, thou hast thy music too,—
While barred clouds bloom the soft-dying day,
  And touch the stubble-plains with rosy hue:

Then in a wailful choir the small gnats mourn

  Among the river sallows, borne aloft

    Or sinking as the light wind lives or dies; .

And full-grown lambs loud bleat from hilly bourn; 30

  Hedge-crickets sing; and now with treble soft

  The red-breast whistles from a garden-croft;

    And gathering swallows twitter in the skies.

ODE ON MELANCHOLY.

1.

No, no, go not to Lethe, neither twist
   Wolf's-bane, tight-rooted, for its poisonous wine;
Nor suffer thy pale forehead to be kiss'd
   By nightshade, ruby grape of Proserpine;
Make not your rosary of yew-berries,
   Nor let the beetle, nor the death-moth be
     Your mournful Psyche, nor the downy owl
A partner in your sorrow's mysteries;
   For shade to shade will come too drowsily,
     And drown the wakeful anguish of the soul.   10

2.

But when the melancholy fit shall fall
  Sudden from heaven like a weeping cloud,
That fosters the droop-headed flowers all,
  And hides the green hill in an April shroud ;
Then glut thy sorrow on a morning rose,
  Or on the rainbow of the salt sand-wave.
    Or on the wealth of globed peonies ;
Or if thy mistress some rich anger shows,
  Emprison her soft hand, and let her rave,
    And feed deep, deep upon her peerless eyes. 20

3.

She dwells with Beauty—Beauty that must die ;
  And Joy, whose hand is ever at his lips
Bidding adieu ; and aching Pleasure nigh,
  Turning to poison while the bee-mouth sips :

Ay, in the very temple of Delight
  Veil'd Melancholy has her sovran shrine,
    Though seen of none save him whose strenuous
      tongue
Can burst Joy's grape against his palate fine;
  His soul shall taste the sadness of her might,
    And be among her cloudy trophies hung.   30

HYPERION.

A FRAGMENT.

HYPERION.

———

BOOK I.

DEEP in the shady sadness of a vale
Far sunken from the healthy breath of morn,
Far from the fiery noon, and eve's one star,
Sat gray-hair'd Saturn, quiet as a stone,
Still as the silence round about his lair;
Forest on forest hung about his head
Like cloud on cloud. No stir of air was there,
Not so much life as on a summer's day
Robs not one light seed from the feather'd grass,
But where the dead leaf fell, there did it rest.   10

A stream went voiceless by, still deadened more
By reason of his fallen divinity
Spreading a shade : the Naiad 'mid her reeds
Press'd her cold finger closer to her lips.

Along the margin-sand large foot-marks went,
No further than to where his feet had stray'd,
And slept there since.   Upon the sodden ground
His old right hand lay nerveless, listless, dead,
Unsceptred ; and his realmless eyes were closed ;
While his bow'd head seem'd list'ning to the Earth, 20
His ancient mother, for some comfort yet.

It seem'd no force could wake him from his place ;
But there came one, who with a kindred hand
Touch'd his wide shoulders, after bending low
With reverence, though to one who knew it not.
She was a Goddess of the infant world ;

By her in stature the tall Amazon

Had stood a pigmy's height: she would have ta'en

Achilles by the hair and bent his neck;

Or with a finger stay'd Ixion's wheel.　　　30

Her face was large as that of Memphian sphinx,

Pedestal'd haply in a palace court,

When sages look'd to Egypt for their lore.

But oh! how unlike marble was that face:

How beautiful, if sorrow had not made

Sorrow more beautiful than Beauty's self.

There was a listening fear in her regard,

As if calamity had but begun;

As if the vanward clouds of evil days

Had spent their malice, and the sullen rear　　　40

Was with its stored thunder labouring up.

One hand she press'd upon that aching spot

Where beats the human heart, as if just there,

Though an immortal, she felt cruel pain:

L 2

The other upon Saturn's bended neck
She laid, and to the level of his ear
Leaning with parted lips, some words she spake
In solemn tenour and deep organ tone :
Some mourning words, which in our feeble tongue
Would come in these like accents ; O how frail 50
To that large utterance of the early Gods !
" Saturn, look up !—though wherefore, poor old King?
" I have no comfort for thee, no not one :
" I cannot say, ' O wherefore sleepest thou ? '
" For heaven is parted from thee, and the earth
" Knows thee not, thus afflicted, for a God ;
" And ocean too, with all its solemn noise,
" Has from thy sceptre pass'd ; and all the air
" Is emptied of thine hoary majesty.
" Thy thunder, conscious of the new command, 60
" Rumbles reluctant o'er our fallen house ;
" And thy sharp lightning in unpractised hands

" Scorches and burns our once serene domain.

" O aching time ! O moments big as years !

" All as ye pass swell out the monstrous truth,

" And press it so upon our weary griefs

" That unbelief has not a space to breathe.

" Saturn, sleep on :—O thoughtless, why did I

" Thus violate thy slumbrous solitude ?

" Why should I ope thy melancholy eyes ?   70

" Saturn, sleep on ! while at thy feet I weep."

    As when, upon a tranced summer-night,

Those green-rob'd senators of mighty woods,

Tall oaks, branch-charmed by the earnest stars,

Dream, and so dream all night without a stir,

Save from one gradual solitary gust

Which comes upon the silence, and dies off,

As if the ebbing air had but one wave ;

So came these words and went ; the while in tears

She touch'd her fair large forehead to the ground, 80
Just where her falling hair might be outspread
A soft and silken mat for Saturn's feet.
One moon, with alteration slow, had shed
Her silver seasons four upon the night,
And still these two were postured motionless,
Like natural sculpture in cathedral cavern;
The frozen God still couchant on the earth,
And the sad Goddess weeping at his feet:
Until at length old Saturn lifted up
His faded eyes, and saw his kingdom gone,   90
And all the gloom and sorrow of the place,
And that fair kneeling Goddess; and then spake,
As with a palsied tongue, and while his beard
Shook horrid with such aspen-malady:
" O tender spouse of gold Hyperion,
" Thea, I feel thee ere I see thy face;
" Look up, and let me see our doom in it;

" Look up, and tell me if this feeble shape

" Is Saturn's ; tell me, if thou hear'st the voice

" Of Saturn ; tell me, if this wrinkling brow,   100

" Naked and bare of its great diadem,

" Peers like the front of Saturn.   Who had power

" To make me desolate ? whence came the strength ?

" How was it nurtur'd to such bursting forth,

" While Fate seem'd strangled in my nervous grasp ?

" But it is so ; and I am smother'd up,

" And buried from all godlike exercise

" Of influence benign on planets pale,

" Of admonitions to the winds and seas,

" Of peaceful sway above man's harvesting,   110

" And all those acts which Deity supreme

" Doth ease its heart of love in.—I am gone

" Away from my own bosom : I have left

" My strong identity, my real self,

" Somewhere between the throne, and where I sit

" Here on this spot of earth.   Search, Thea, search !

" Open thine eyes eterne, and sphere them round

" Upon all space : space starr'd, and lorn of light ;

" Space region'd with life-air ; and barren void ;

" Spaces of fire, and all the yawn of hell.—   120

" Search, Thea, search ! and tell me, if thou seest

" A certain shape or shadow, making way

" With wings or chariot fierce to repossess

" A heaven he lost erewhile : it must—it must

" Be of ripe progress—Saturn must be King.

" Yes, there must be a golden victory ;

" There must be Gods thrown down, and trumpets blown

" Of triumph calm, and hymns of festival

" Upon the gold clouds metropolitan,

" Voices of soft proclaim, and silver stir   130

" Of strings in hollow shells ; and there shall be

" Beautiful things made new, for the surprise

" Of the sky-children ; I will give command :

" Thea ! Thea ! Thea ! where is Saturn ? "

This passion lifted him upon his feet,

And made his hands to struggle in the air,

His Druid locks to shake and ooze with sweat,

His eyes to fever out, his voice to cease.

He stood, and heard not Thea's sobbing deep;

A little time, and then again he snatch'd   140

Utterance thus.—" But cannot I create ?

" Cannot I form ? Cannot I fashion forth

" Another world, another universe,

" To overbear and crumble this to nought ?

" Where is another chaos ? Where ? "—That word

Found way unto Olympus, and made quake

The rebel three.—Thea was startled up,

And in her bearing was a sort of hope,

As thus she quick-voic'd spake, yet full of awe.

"This cheers our fallen house : come to our friends, 150

" O Saturn ! come away, and give them heart ;

" I know the covert, for thence came I hither."
Thus brief ; then with beseeching eyes she went
With backward footing through the shade a space :
He follow'd, and she turn'd to lead the way
Through aged boughs, that yielded like the mist
Which eagles cleave upmounting from their nest.

  Meanwhile in other realms big tears were shed,
More sorrow like to this, and such like woe,
Too huge for mortal tongue or pen of scribe :   160
The Titans fierce, self-hid, or prison-bound,
Groan'd for the old allegiance once more,
And listen'd in sharp pain for Saturn's voice.
But one of the whole mammoth-brood still kept
His sov'reignty, and rule, and majesty ;—
Blazing Hyperion on his orbed fire
Still sat, still snuff'd the incense, teeming up
From man to the sun's God ; yet unsecure :

For as among us mortals omens drear
Fright and perplex, so also shuddered he—   170
Not at dog's howl, or gloom-bird's hated screech,
Or the familiar visiting of one
Upon the first toll of his passing-bell,
Or prophesyings of the midnight lamp;
But horrors, portion'd to a giant nerve,
Oft made Hyperion ache. His palace bright
Bastion'd with pyramids of glowing gold,
And touch'd with shade of bronzed obelisks,
Glar'd a blood-red through all its thousand courts,
Arches, and domes, and fiery galleries;   180
And all its curtains of Aurorian clouds
Flush'd angerly: while sometimes eagle's wings,
Unseen before by Gods or wondering men,
Darken'd the place; and neighing steeds were heard,
Not heard before by Gods or wondering men.
Also, when he would taste the spicy wreaths

Of incense, breath'd aloft from sacred hills,

Instead of sweets, his ample palate took

Savour of poisonous brass and metal sick:

And so, when harbour'd in the sleepy west,   190

After the full completion of fair day,—

For rest divine upon exalted couch

And slumber in the arms of melody,

He pac'd away the pleasant hours of ease

With stride colossal, on from hall to hall;

While far within each aisle and deep recess,

His winged minions in close clusters stood,

Amaz'd and full of fear; like anxious men

Who on wide plains gather in panting troops,

When earthquakes jar their battlements and towers. 200

Even now, while Saturn, rous'd from icy trance,

Went step for step with Thea through the woods,

Hyperion, leaving twilight in the rear,

Came slope upon the threshold of the west;

Then, as was wont, his palace-door flew ope
In smoothest silence, save what solemn tubes,
Blown by the serious Zephyrs, gave of sweet
And wandering sounds, slow-breathed melodies;
And like a rose in vermeil tint and shape,
In fragrance soft, and coolness to the eye,   210
That inlet to severe magnificence
Stood full blown, for the God to enter in.

　He enter'd, but he enter'd full of wrath;
His flaming robes stream'd out beyond his heels,
And gave a roar, as if of earthly fire,
That scar'd away the meek ethereal Hours
And made their dove-wings tremble.　On he flared,
From stately nave to nave, from vault to vault,
Through bowers of fragrant and enwreathed light,
And diamond-paved lustrous long arcades,   220

Until he reach'd the great main cupola;

There standing fierce beneath, he stampt his foot,

And from the basements deep to the high towers

Jarr'd his own golden region; and before

The quavering thunder thereupon had ceas'd,

His voice leapt out, despite of godlike curb,

To this result: " O dreams of day and night!

" O monstrous forms! O effigies of pain!

" O spectres busy in a cold, cold gloom!

" O lank-eared Phantoms of black-weeded pools! 230

" Why do I know ye? why have I seen ye? why

" Is my eternal essence thus distraught

" To see and to behold these horrors new?

" Saturn is fallen, am I too to fall?

" Am I to leave this haven of my rest,

" This cradle of my glory, this soft clime,

" This calm luxuriance of blissful light,

" These crystalline pavilions, and pure fanes,

" Of all my lucent empire ? It is left

" Deserted, void, nor any haunt of mine. 240

" The blaze, the splendor, and the symmetry.

" I cannot see—but darkness, death and darkness.

" Even here, into my centre of repose,

" The shady visions come to domineer,

" Insult, and blind, and stifle up my pomp.—

" Fall !—No, by Tellus and her briny robes !

" Over the fiery frontier of my realms

" I will advance a terrible right arm

" Shall scare that infant thunderer, rebel Jove,

" And bid old Saturn take his throne again."— 250

He spake, and ceas'd, the while a heavier threat

Held struggle with his throat but came not forth ;

For as in theatres of crowded men

Hubbub increases more they call out " Hush ! "

So at Hyperion's words the Phantoms pale

Bestirr'd themselves, thrice horrible and cold ;

And from the mirror'd level where he stood
A mist arose, as from a scummy marsh.
At this, through all his bulk an agony
Crept gradual, from the feet unto the crown,   260
Like a lithe serpent vast and muscular
Making slow way, with head and neck convuls'd
From over-strained might.   Releas'd, he fled
To the eastern gates, and full six dewy hours
Before the dawn in season due should blush,
He breath'd fierce breath against the sleepy portals,
Clear'd them of heavy vapours, burst them wide
Suddenly on the ocean's chilly streams.
The planet orb of fire, whereon he rode
Each day from east to west the heavens through, 270
Spun round in sable curtaining of clouds;
Not therefore veiled quite, blindfold, and hid,
But ever and anon the glancing spheres,
Circles, and arcs, and broad-belting colure,

Glow'd through, and wrought upon the muffling dark

Sweet-shaped lightnings from the nadir deep

Up to the zenith,—hieroglyphics old,

Which sages and keen-eyed astrologers

Then living on the earth, with labouring thought

Won from the gaze of many centuries :　　　280

Now lost, save what we find on remnants huge

Of stone, or marble swart ; their import gone,

Their wisdom long since fled.—Two wings this orb

Possess'd for glory, two fair argent wings,

Ever exalted at the God's approach ·

And now, from forth the gloom their plumes immense

Rose, one by one, till all outspreaded were ;

While still the dazzling globe maintain'd eclipse,

Awaiting for Hyperion's command.

Fain would he have commanded, fain took throne 290

And bid the day begin, if but for change.

He might not :—No, though a primeval God :

1082·2　　　　　　　M

The sacred seasons might not be disturb'd.

Therefore the operations of the dawn

Stay'd in their birth, even as here 'tis told.

Those silver wings expanded sisterly,

Eager to sail their orb; the porches wide

Open'd upon the dusk demesnes of night

And the bright Titan, phrenzied with new woes,

Unus'd to bend, by hard compulsion bent   300

His spirit to the sorrow of the time;

And all along a dismal rack of clouds,

Upon the boundaries of day and night,

He stretch'd himself in grief and radiance faint.

There as he lay, the Heaven with its stars

Look'd down on him with pity, and the voice

Of Cœlus, from the universal space,

Thus whisper'd low and solemn in his ear.

" O brightest of my children dear, earth-born

" And sky-engendered, Son of Mysteries   310

" All unrevealed even to the powers

" Which met at thy creating; at whose joys

" And palpitations sweet, and pleasures soft,

" I, Cœlus, wonder, how they came and whence;

" And at the fruits thereof what shapes they be,

" Distinct, and visible; symbols divine,

" Manifestations of that beauteous life

" Diffus'd unseen throughout eternal space:

" Of these new-form'd art thou, oh brightest child!

" Of these, thy brethren and the Goddesses!   320

" There is sad feud among ye, and rebellion

" Of son against his sire. I saw him fall,

" I saw my first-born tumbled from his throne!

" To me his arms were spread, to me his voice

" Found way from forth the thunders round his head!

" Pale wox I, and in vapours hid my face.

" Art thou, too, near such doom? vague fear there is:

" For I have seen my sons most unlike Gods.

M 2

" Divine ye were created, and divine

" In sad demeanour, solemn, undisturb'd,   330

" Unruffled, like high Gods, ye liv'd and ruled :

" Now I behold in you fear, hope, and wrath ;

" Actions of rage and passion ; even as

" I see them, on the mortal world beneath,

" In men who die.—This is the grief, O Son !

" Sad sign of ruin, sudden dismay, and fall !

" Yet do thou strive ; as thou art capable,

" As thou canst move about, an evident God ;

" And canst oppose to each malignant hour

" Ethereal presence :—I am but a voice ;   340

" My life is but the life of winds and tides,

" No more than winds and tides can I avail :—

" But thou canst.—Be thou therefore in the van

" Of circumstance ; yea, seize the arrow's barb

" Before the tense string murmur.—To the earth !

" For there thou wilt find Saturn, and his woes.

" Meantime **I will** keep watch on thy bright sun,

" **And** of thy seasons be a careful nurse."—

Ere half this region-whisper had come down,

Hyperion arose, and on the stars   350

Lifted his curved lids, and kept them wide

Until it ceas'd ; and still he kept them wide :

And still they were the same bright, patient stars.

Then with a slow incline of his broad breast,

Like to a diver in the pearly seas,

Forward he stoop'd over the airy shore,

And plung'd all noiseless into the deep night.

HYPERION.

BOOK II.

JUST at the self-same beat of Time's wide wings
Hyperion slid into the rustled air,
And Saturn gain'd with Thea that sad place
Where Cybele and the bruised Titans mourn'd.
It was a den where no insulting light
Could glimmer on their tears; where their own groans
They felt, but heard not, for the solid roar
Of thunderous waterfalls and torrents hoarse,
Pouring a constant bulk, uncertain where.
Crag jutting forth to crag, and rocks that seem'd 10

Ever as if just rising from a sleep,

Forehead to forehead held their monstrous horns;

And thus in thousand hugest phantasies

Made a fit roofing to this nest of woe.

Instead of thrones, hard flint they sat upon,

Couches of rugged stone, and slaty ridge

Stubborn'd with iron. All were not assembled:

Some chain'd in torture, and some wandering.

Cœus, and Gyges, and Briareüs,

Typhon, and Dolor, and Porphyrion,   20

With many more, the brawniest in assault,

Were pent in regions of laborious breath;

Dungeon'd in opaque element, to keep

Their clenched teeth still clench'd, and all their limbs

Lock'd up like veins of metal, crampt and screw'd;

Without a motion, save of their big hearts

Heaving in pain, and horribly convuls'd

With sanguine feverous boiling gurge of pulse.

Mnemosyne was straying in the world;

Far from her moon had Phœbe wandered;   30

And many else were free to roam abroad,

But for the main, here found they covert drear.

Scarce images of life, one here, one there,

Lay vast and edgeways; like a dismal cirque

Of Druid stones, upon a forlorn moor,

When the chill rain begins at shut of eve,

In dull November, and their chancel vault,

The Heaven itself, is blinded throughout night.

Each one kept shroud, nor to his neighbour gave

Or word, or look, or action of despair.   40

Creüs was one; his ponderous iron mace

Lay by him, and a shatter'd rib of rock

Told of his rage, ere he thus sank and pined.

Iäpetus another; in his grasp,

A serpent's plashy neck; its barbed tongue

Squeez'd from the gorge, and all its uncurl'd length

Dead ; and because the creature could not spit

Its poison in the eyes of conquering Jove.

Next Cottus : prone he lay, chin uppermost,

As though in pain ; for still upon the flint   50

He ground severe his skull, with open mouth

And eyes at horrid working. Nearest him

Asia, born of most enormous Caf,

Who cost her mother Tellus keener pangs,

Though feminine, than any of her sons :

More thought than woe was in her dusky face,

For she was prophesying of her glory ;

And in her wide imagination stood

Palm-shaded temples, and high rival fanes,

By Oxus or in Ganges' sacred isles.   60

Even as Hope upon her anchor leans,

So leant she, not so fair, upon a tusk

Shed from the broadest of her elephants.

Above her, on a crag's uneasy shelve.

Upon his elbow rais'd, all prostrate else,
Shadow'd Enceladus; once tame and mild
As grazing ox unworried in the meads;
Now tiger-passion'd, lion-thoughted, wroth,
He meditated, plotted, and even now
Was hurling mountains in that second war,   70
Not long delay'd, that scar'd the younger Gods
To hide themselves in forms of beast and bird.
Not far hence Atlas; and beside him prone
Phorcus, the sire of Gorgons. Neighbour'd close
Oceanus, and Tethys, in whose lap
Sobb'd Clymene among her tangled hair.
In midst of all lay Themis, at the feet
Of Ops the queen all clouded round from sight;
No shape distinguishable, more than when
Thick night confounds the pine-tops with the clouds : 80
And many else whose names may not be told.
For when the Muse's wings are air-ward spread,

Who shall delay her flight ? And she must chaunt
Of Saturn, and his guide, who now had climb'd
With damp and slippery footing from a depth
More horrid still.   Above a sombre cliff
Their heads appear'd, and up their stature grew
Till on the level height their steps found ease :
Then Thea spread abroad her trembling arms
Upon the precincts of this nest of pain,   90
And sidelong fix'd her eye on Saturn's face :
There saw she direst strife ; the supreme God
At war with all the frailty of grief,
Of rage, of fear, anxiety, revenge,
Remorse, spleen, hope, but most of all despair.
Against these plagues he strove in vain ; for Fate
Had pour'd a mortal oil upon his head,
A disanointing poison : so that Thea,
Affrighted, kept her still, and let him pass
First onwards in, among the fallen tribe.   100

As with us mortal men, the laden heart
Is persecuted more, and fever'd more,
When it is nighing to the mournful house
Where other hearts are sick of the same bruise;
So Saturn, as he walk'd into the midst,
Felt faint, and would have sunk among the rest,
But that he met Enceladus's eye,
Whose mightiness, and awe of him, at once
Came like an inspiration; and he shouted,
"Titans, behold your God!" at which some groan'd; 110
Some started on their feet; some also shouted;
Some wept, some wail'd, all bow'd with reverence;
And Ops, uplifting her black folded veil,
Show'd her pale cheeks, and all her forehead wan,
Her eye-brows thin and jet, and hollow eyes.
There is a roaring in the bleak-grown pines
When Winter lifts his voice; there is a noise
Among immortals when a God gives sign,

With hushing finger, how he means to load
His tongue with the full weight of utterless thought, 120
With thunder, and with music, and with pomp:
Such noise is like the roar of bleak-grown pines;
Which, when it ceases in this mountain'd world,
No other sound succeeds; but ceasing here,
Among these fallen, Saturn's voice therefrom
Grew up like organ, that begins anew
Its strain, when other harmonies, stopt short,
Leave the dinn'd air vibrating silverly.
Thus grew it up—" Not in my own sad breast,
" Which is its own great judge and searcher out, 130
" Can I find reason why ye should be thus:
" Not in the legends of the first of days,
" Studied from that old spirit-leaved book
" Which starry Uranus with finger bright
" Sav'd from the shores of darkness, when the waves
" Low-ebb'd still hid it up in shallow gloom;—

" And the which book ye know I ever kept

" For my firm-based footstool :—Ah, infirm !

" Not there, nor in sign, symbol, or portent

" Of element, earth, water, air, and fire,—　　140

" At war, at peace, or inter-quarreling

" One against one, or two, or three, or all

" Each several one against the other three,

" As fire with air loud warring when rain-floods

" Drown both, and press them both against earth's face.

" Where, finding sulphur, a quadruple wrath

" Unhinges the poor world ;—not in that strife,

" Wherefrom I take strange lore, and read it deep,

" Can I find reason why ye should be thus :

" No, no-where can unriddle, though I search,　　150

" And pore on Nature's universal scroll

" Even to swooning, why ye, Divinities,

" The first-born of all shap'd and palpable Gods,

" Should cower beneath what, in comparison,

" Is untremendous might. Yet ye are here,

" O'erwhelm'd, and spurn'd, and batter'd, ye are here !

" O Titans, shall I say ' Arise ! '—Ye groan :

" Shall I say ' Crouch ! '—Ye groan. What can I then?

" O Heaven wide ! O unseen parent dear !

" What can I ? Tell me, all ye brethren Gods,   160

" How we can war, how engine our great wrath !

" O speak your counsel now, for Saturn's ear

" Is all a-hunger'd. Thou, Oceanus,

" Ponderest high and deep ; and in thy face

" I see, astonied, that severe content

" Which comes of thought and musing : give us help ! "

So ended Saturn ; and the God of the Sea,

Sophist and sage, from no Athenian grove,

But cogitation in his watery shades,

Arose, with locks not oozy, and began,   170

In murmurs, which his first-endeavouring tongue

Caught infant-like from the far-foamed sands.

" O ye, whom wrath consumes ! who, passion-stung,

" Writhe at defeat, and nurse your agonies !

" Shut up your senses, stifle up your ears,

" My voice is not a bellows unto ire.

" Yet listen, ye who will, whilst I bring proof

" How ye, perforce, must be content to stoop :

" And in the proof much comfort will I give,

" If ye will take that comfort in its truth.　　180

" We fall by course of Nature's law, not force

" Of thunder, or of Jove.　Great Saturn, thou

" Hast sifted well the atom-universe ;

" But for this reason, that thou art the King,

" And only blind from sheer supremacy,

" One avenue was shaded from thine eyes,

" Through which I wandered to eternal truth.

" And first, as thou wast not the first of powers,

" So art thou not the last ; it cannot be :

" Thou art not the beginning nor the end.   190

" From chaos and parental darkness came

" Light, the first fruits of that intestine broil,

" That sullen ferment, which for wondrous ends

" Was ripening in itself.   The ripe hour came,

" And with it light, and light, engendering

" Upon its own producer, forthwith touch'd

" The whole enormous matter into life.

" Upon that very hour, our parentage,

" The Heavens and the Earth, were manifest :

" Then thou first-born, and we the giant-race,   200

" Found ourselves ruling new and beauteous realms.

" Now comes the pain of truth, to whom 'tis pain ;

" O folly ! for to bear all naked truths,

" And to envisage circumstance, all calm,

" That is the top of sovereignty.   Mark well !

" As Heaven and Earth are fairer, fairer far

" Than Chaos and blank Darkness, though once chiefs ;

" And as we show beyond that Heaven and Earth

" In form and shape compact and beautiful,

" In will, in action free, companionship,   210

" And thousand other signs of purer life ;

" So on our heels a fresh perfection treads,

" A power more strong in beauty, born of us

" And fated to excel us, as we pass

" In glory that old Darkness : nor are we

" Thereby more conquer'd, than by us the rule

" Of shapeless Chaos. Say, doth the dull soil

" Quarrel with the proud forests it hath fed,

" And feedeth still, more comely than itself ?

" Can it deny the chiefdom of green groves ?   220

" Or shall the tree be envious of the dove

" Because it cooeth, and hath snowy wings

" To wander wherewithal and find its joys ?

" We are such forest-trees, and our fair boughs

" Have bred forth, not pale solitary doves,

" But eagles golden-feather'd, who do tower

" Above us in their beauty, and must reign

" In right thereof ; for 'tis the eternal law

" That first in beauty should be first in might :

" Yea, by that law, another race may drive   230

" Our conquerors to mourn as we do now.

" Have ye beheld the young God of the Seas,

" My dispossessor ? Have ye seen his face ?

" Have ye beheld his chariot, foam'd along

" By noble winged creatures he hath made ?

" I saw him on the calmed waters scud,

" With such a glow of beauty in his eyes,

" That it enforc'd me to bid sad farewell

" To all my empire : farewell sad I took,

" And hither came, to see how dolorous fate   240

" Had wrought upon ye ; and how I might best

" Give consolation in this woe extreme.

" Receive the truth, and let it be your balm."

prestles

   Whether through poz'd conviction, or disdain,

They guarded silence, when Oceanus

Left murmuring, what deepest thought can tell ?

But so it was, none answer'd for a space,

Save one whom none regarded, Clymene ;

And yet she answer'd not, only complain'd,

With hectic lips, and eyes up-looking mild,   250

Thus wording timidly among the fierce :

" O Father, I am here the simplest voice,

" And all my knowledge is that joy is gone,

" And this thing woe crept in among our hearts,

" There to remain for ever, as I fear :

" I would not bode of evil, if I thought

" So weak a creature could turn off the help

" Which by just right should come of mighty Gods ;

" Yet let me tell my sorrow, let me tell

" Of what I heard, and how it made me weep,   260

" And know that we had parted from all hope.

" I stood upon a shore, a pleasant shore,

" Where a sweet clime was breathed from a land

" Of fragrance, quietness, and trees, and flowers.

" Full of calm joy it was, as I of grief ;

" Too full of joy and soft delicious warmth ;

" So that I felt a movement in my heart

" To chide, and to reproach that solitude

" With songs of misery, music of our woes ;

" And sat me down, and took a mouthed shell 270

" And murmur'd into it, and made melody—

" O melody no more ! for while I sang,

" And with poor skill let pass into the breeze

" The dull shell's echo, from a bowery strand

" Just opposite, an island of the sea,

" There came enchantment with the shifting wind,

" That did both drown and keep alive my ears.

" I threw my shell away upon the sand,

" And a wave fill'd it, as my sense was fill'd

Music much sweeter than the could make

Apollo

God of Music

" With that new blissful golden melody.   280

" A living death was in each gush of sounds,

" Each family of rapturous hurried notes,

" That fell, one after one, yet all at once,

" Like pearl beads dropping sudden from their string :

" And then another, then another strain,

" Each like a dove leaving its olive perch,

" With music wing'd instead of silent plumes,

" To hover round my head, and make me sick

" Of joy and grief at once.   Grief overcame,

" And I was stopping up my frantic ears,   290

" When, past all hindrance of my trembling hands,

" A voice came sweeter, sweeter than all tune,

" And still it cried, ' Apollo ! young Apollo !

" ' The morning-bright Apollo ! young Apollo ! '

" I fled, it follow'd me, and cried ' Apollo ! '

" O Father, and O Brethren, had ye felt

" Those pains of mine ; O Saturn, hadst thou felt,

" Ye would not call this too indulged tongue

" Presumptuous, in thus venturing to be heard."

  So far her voice flow'd on, like timorous brook 300

That, lingering along a pebbled coast,

Doth fear to meet the sea : but sea it met,

And shudder'd ; for the overwhelming voice

Of huge Enceladus swallow'd it in wrath :

The ponderous syllables, like sullen waves

In the half-glutted hollows of reef-rocks,

Came booming thus, while still upon his arm

He lean'd ; not rising, from supreme contempt.

" Or shall we listen to the over-wise,   *Oceanus*

" Or to the over-foolish, Giant-Gods ?   *Clymene*   310

" Not thunderbolt on thunderbolt, till all

" That rebel Jove's whole armoury were spent,

" Not world on world upon these shoulders piled,

" Could agonize me more than baby-words

" In midst of this dethronement horrible.

" Speak! roar! shout! yell! ye sleepy Titans all.

" Do ye forget the blows, the buffets vile?

" Are ye not smitten by a youngling arm?

" Dost thou forget, sham Monarch of the Waves,

" Thy scalding in the seas? What, have I rous'd　320

" Your spleens with so few simple words as these?

" O joy! for now I see ye are not lost:

" O joy! for now I see a thousand eyes

" Wide glaring for revenge!"—As this he said,

He lifted up his stature vast, and stood,

Still without intermission speaking thus:

" Now ye are flames, I'll tell you how to burn,

" And purge the ether of our enemies;

' How to feed fierce the crooked stings of fire,

" And singe away the swollen clouds of Jove,　330

" Stifling that puny essence in its tent.

" O let him feel the evil he hath done;

" For though I scorn Oceanus's lore,

" Much pain have I for more than loss of realms :

" The days of peace and slumberous calm are fled ;

" Those days, all innocent of scathing war,

" When all the fair Existences of heaven

" Came open-eyed to guess what we would speak :—

" That was before our brows were taught to frown,

" Before our lips knew else but solemn sounds ; 340

" That was before we knew the winged thing,

" Victory, might be lost, or might be won.

" And be ye mindful that Hyperion,

" Our brightest brother, still is undisgraced—

" Hyperion, lo ! his radiance is here ! "

All eyes were on Enceladus's face,

And they beheld, while still Hyperion's name

Flew from his lips up to the vaulted rocks,

A pallid gleam across his features stern :

Not savage, for he saw full many a God   350

Wroth as himself. He look'd upon them all,

And in each face he saw a gleam of light,

But splendider in Saturn's, whose hoar locks

Shone like the bubbling foam about a keel

When the prow sweeps into a midnight cove.

In pale and silver silence they remain'd,

Till suddenly a splendour, like the morn,

Pervaded all the beetling gloomy steeps,

All the sad spaces of oblivion,

And every gulf, and every chasm old,   360

And every height, and every sullen depth,

Voiceless, or hoarse with loud tormented streams:

And all the everlasting cataracts,

And all the headlong torrents far and near,

Mantled before in darkness and huge shade,

Now saw the light and made it terrible.

It was Hyperion :—a granite peak

His bright feet touch'd, and there he stay'd to view

The misery his brilliance had betray'd

To the most hateful seeing of itself.   370

Golden his hair of short Numidian curl,

Regal his shape majestic, a vast shade

In midst of his own brightness, like the bulk

Of Memnon's image at the set of sun

To one who travels from the dusking East:

Sighs, too, as mournful as that Memnon's harp

He utter'd, while his hands contemplative

He press'd together, and in silence stood.

Despondence seiz'd again the fallen Gods

At sight of the dejected King of Day,   380

And many hid their faces from the light:

But fierce Enceladus sent forth his eyes

Among the brotherhood; and, at their glare,

Uprose Iäpetus, and Creüs too,

And Phorcus, sea-born, and together strode

To where he towered on his eminence.

There those four shouted forth old Saturn's name ;

Hyperion from the peak loud answered, " Saturn ! "

Saturn sat near the Mother of the Gods,

In whose face was no joy, though all the Gods 390

Gave from their hollow throats the name of " Saturn !"

HYPERION.

BOOK III.

THUS in alternate uproar and sad peace,

Amazed were those Titans utterly.

O leave them, Muse! O leave them to their woes;

For thou art weak to sing such tumults dire:

A solitary sorrow best befits

Thy lips, and antheming a lonely grief.

Leave them, O Muse! for thou anon wilt find

Many a fallen old Divinity

Wandering in vain about bewildered shores.

Meantime touch piously the Delphic harp,   10

And not a wind of heaven but will breathe

In aid soft warble from the Dorian flute;

For lo! 'tis for the Father of all verse.

Flush every thing that hath a vermeil hue,

Let the rose glow intense and warm the air,

And let the clouds of even and of morn

Float in voluptuous fleeces o'er the hills;

Let the red wine within the goblet boil,

Cold as a bubbling well; let faint-lipp'd shells,

On sands, or in great deeps, vermilion turn   20

Through all their labyrinths; and let the maid

Blush keenly, as with some warm kiss surpris'd.

Chief isle of the embowered Cyclades,

Rejoice, O Delos, with thine olives green,

And poplars, and lawn-shading palms, and beech,

In which the Zephyr breathes the loudest song,

And hazels thick, dark-stemm'd beneath the shade:

Apollo is once more the golden theme!

Where was he, when the Giant of the Sun
Stood bright, amid the sorrow of his peers ? 30
Together had he left his mother fair
And his twin-sister sleeping in their bower,
And in the morning twilight wandered forth
Beside the osiers of a rivulet,
Full ankle-deep in lilies of the vale.
The nightingale had ceas'd, and a few stars
Were lingering in the heavens, while the thrush
Began calm-throated. Throughout all the isle
There was no covert, no retired cave
Unhaunted by the murmurous noise of waves, 40
Though scarcely heard in many a green recess.
He listen'd, and he wept, and his bright tears
Went trickling down the golden bow he held.
Thus with half-shut suffused eyes he stood,
While from beneath some cumbrous boughs hard by

With solemn step an awful Goddess came,

And there was purport in her looks for him,

Which he with eager guess began to read

Perplex'd, the while melodiously he said :

" How cam'st thou over the unfooted sea ?   50

" Or hath that antique mien and robed form

" Mov'd in these vales invisible till now ?

" Sure I have heard those vestments sweeping o'er

" The fallen leaves, when I have sat alone

" In cool mid-forest. Surely I have traced

" The rustle of those ample skirts about

" These grassy solitudes, and seen the flowers

" Lift up their heads, as still the whisper pass'd.

" Goddess ! I have beheld those eyes before,

" And their eternal calm, and all that face,   60

" Or I have dream'd."—" Yes," said the supreme shape,

" Thou hast dream'd of me ; and awaking up

" Didst find a lyre all golden by thy side,

" Whose strings touch'd by thy fingers, all the vast

" Unwearied ear of the whole universe

" Listen'd in pain and pleasure at the birth

" Of such new tuneful wonder. Is't not strange

" That thou shouldst weep, so gifted ? Tell me, youth,

" What sorrow thou canst feel ; for I am sad

" When thou dost shed a tear : explain thy griefs 70

" To one who in this lonely isle hath been

" The watcher of thy sleep and hours of life,

" From the young day when first thy infant hand

" Pluck'd witless the weak flowers, till thine arm

" Could bend that bow heroic to all times.

" Show thy heart's secret to an ancient Power

" Who hath forsaken old and sacred thrones

" For prophecies of thee, and for the sake

" Of loveliness new born."—Apollo then,

With sudden scrutiny and gloomless eyes,   80

Thus answer'd, while his white melodious throat

Throbb'd with the syllables.—" Mnemosyne !

" Thy name is on my tongue, I know not how ;

" Why should I tell thee what thou so well seest ?

" Why should I strive to show what from thy lips

" Would come no mystery ? For me, dark, dark,

" And painful vile oblivion seals my eyes :

" I strive to search wherefore I am so sad,

" Until a melancholy numbs my limbs ;

" And then upon the grass I sit, and moan,   90

" Like one who once had wings.—O why should I

" Feel curs'd and thwarted, when the liegeless air

" Yields to my step aspirant ? why should I

" Spurn the green turf as hateful to my feet ?

" Goddess benign, point forth some unknown thing :

" Are there not other regions than this isle ?

" What are the stars ? There is the sun, the sun !

" And the most patient brilliance of the moon !

" And stars by thousands ! Point me out the way

" To any one particular beauteous star,　　　100

" And I will flit into it with my lyre,

" And make its silvery splendour pant with bliss.

" I have heard the cloudy thunder : Where is power ?

" Whose hand, whose essence, what divinity

" Makes this alarum in the elements,

" While I here idle listen on the shores

" In fearless yet in aching ignorance ?

" O tell me, lonely Goddess, by thy harp,

" That waileth every morn and eventide,

" Tell me why thus I rave, about these groves ! 110

" Mute thou remainest—Mute ! yet I can read

" A wondrous lesson in thy silent face :

" Knowledge enormous makes a God of me.

" Names, deeds, gray legends, dire events, rebellions,

" Majesties, sovran voices, agonies.

" Creations and destroyings, all at once

" Pour into the wide hollows of my brain,

" And deify me, as if some blithe wine

" Or bright elixir peerless I had drunk,

" And so become immortal."—Thus the God,   120

While his enkindled eyes, with level glance

Beneath his white soft temples, stedfast kept

Trembling with light upon Mnemosyne.

Soon wild commotions shook him, and made flush

All the immortal fairness of his limbs ;

Most like the struggle at the gate of death ;

Or liker still to one who should take leave

Of pale immortal death, and with a pang

As hot as death's is chill, with fierce convulse

Die into life : so young Apollo anguish'd :   130

His very hair, his golden tresses famed
Kept undulation round his eager neck.
During the pain Mnemosyne upheld
Her arms as one who prophesied.—At length
Apollo shriek'd;—and lo! from all his limbs
Celestial   *   *   *   *   *   *
*   *   *   *   *   *   *   *

glory dawned; he was a god.

THE END

NOTE.

PAGE 184, l. 310.   over-foolish, Giant-Gods ?   *MS.* ;
over-foolish giant, Gods ?   *1820.*

NOTES.

ADVERTISEMENT.

PAGE 2.   See Introduction to *Hyperion*, p. 245.

INTRODUCTION TO LAMIA.

Lamia, like *Endymion*, is written in the heroic couplet,
but the difference in style is very marked.   The influence
of Dryden's narrative-poems (his translations from Boccaccio and Chaucer) is clearly traceable in the metre, style,
and construction of the later poem.   Like Dryden, Keats
now makes frequent use of the Alexandrine, or 6-foot line,
and of the triplet.   He has also restrained the exuberance
of his language and gained force, whilst in imaginative
power and felicity of diction he surpasses anything of
which Dryden was capable.   The flaws in his style are
mainly due to carelessness in the rimes and some question-
able coining of words.   He also occasionally lapses into
the vulgarity and triviality which marred certain of his
early poems.

   The best he gained from his study of Dryden's *Fables*,
a debt perhaps to Chaucer rather than to Dryden, was a
notable advance in constructive power.   In *Lamia* he
shows a very much greater sense of proportion and power
of selection than in his earlier work.   There is, as it were,
more light and shade.

   Thus we find that whenever the occasion demands it his
style rises to supreme force and beauty.   The metamor-

phosis of the serpent, the entry of Lamia and Lycius into
Corinth, the building by Lamia of the Fairy Hall, and her
final withering under the eye of Apollonius—these are
the most important points in the story, and the passages in
which they are described are also the most striking in the
poem.

The allegorical meaning of the story seems to be, that
it is fatal to attempt to separate the sensuous and
emotional life from the life of reason. Philosophy alone
is cold and destructive, but the pleasures of the senses
alone are unreal and unsatisfying. The man who
attempts such a divorce between the two parts of his
nature will fail miserably as did Lycius, who, unable per-
manently to exclude reason, was compelled to face the
death of his illusions, and could not, himself, survive
them.

Of the poem Keats himself says, writing to his brother
in September, 1819: 'I have been reading over a part
of a short poem I have composed lately, called *Lamia*, and
I am certain there is that sort of fire in it that must take
hold of people some way; give them either pleasant or
unpleasant sensation—what they want is a sensation
of some sort.' But to the greatest of Keats's critics,
Charles Lamb, the poem appealed somewhat differently,
for he writes, 'More exuberantly rich in imagery and
painting [than *Isabella*] is the story of *Lamia*. It is of as
gorgeous stuff as ever romance was composed of,' and, after
enumerating the most striking pictures in the poem, he
adds, '[these] are all that fairy-land can do for us.'
Lamia struck his imagination, but his heart was given to
Isabella.

NOTES ON LAMIA.

PART I.

PAGE 3. ll. 1–6. *before the faery broods . . . lawns,* i. e. before mediaeval fairy-lore had superseded classical mythology.

l. 2. *Satyr,* a horned and goat-legged demi-god of the woods.

l. 5. *Dryads,* wood-nymphs, who lived in trees. The life of each terminated with that of the tree over which she presided. Cf. Landor's 'Hamadryad'.

l. 5. *Fauns.* The Roman name corresponding to the Greek Satyr.

l. 7. *Hermes,* or Mercury, the messenger of the Gods. He is always represented with winged shoes, a winged helmet, and a winged staff, bound about with living serpents.

PAGE 4. l. 15. *Tritons,* sea-gods, half-man, half-fish. Cf. Wordsworth, 'Or hear old Triton blow his wreathed horn' (Sonnet—'The World is too much with us').

l. 19. *unknown to any Muse,* beyond the imagination of any poet.

PAGE 5. l. 28. *passion new.* He has often before been to earth on similar errands. Cf. *ever-smitten,* l. 7, also ll. 80–93.

l. 42. *dove-footed.* Cf. note on l. 7.

PAGE 6. l. 46. *cirque-couchant,* lying twisted into a circle. Cf. *wreathed tomb,* l. 38.

l. 47. *gordian,* knotted, from the famous knot in the

harness of Gordius, King of Phrygia, which only the conqueror of the world was to be able to undo. Alexander cut it with his sword. Cf. *Henry V*, I. i. 46.

l. 58. *Ariadne's tiar.* Ariadne was a nymph beloved of Bacchus, the god of wine. He gave her a crown of seven stars, which, after her death, was made into a constellation. Keats has, no doubt, in his mind Titian's picture of Bacchus and Ariadne in the National Gallery. Cf. *Ode to Sorrow, Endymion.*

PAGE 7. l. 63. *As Proserpine . . . air.* Proserpine, gathering flowers in the Vale of Enna, in Sicily, was carried off by Pluto, the king of the underworld, to be his queen. Cf. *Winter's Tale*, IV. iii, and *Paradise Lost*, iv. 268, known to be a favourite passage with Keats.

l. 75. *his throbbing . . . moan.* Cf. *Hyperion*, iii. 81.

l. 77. *as morning breaks*, the freshness and splendour of the youthful god.

PAGE 8. l. 78. *Phoebean dart*, a ray of the sun, Phoebus being the god of the sun.

l. 80. *Too gentle Hermes.* Cf. l. 28 and note.

l. 81. *not delay'd* : classical construction. See Introduction to *Hyperion.*

Star of Lethe. Hermes is so called because he had to lead the souls of the dead to Hades, where was Lethe, the river of forgetfulness. Lamb comments: '. . . Hermes, the *Star of Lethe*, as he is called by one of those prodigal phrases which Mr. Keats abounds in, which are each a poem in a word, and which in this instance lays open to us at once, like a picture, all the dim regions and their habitants, and the sudden coming of a celestial among them.'

l. 91. The line dances along like a leaf before the wind.

l. 92. Miltonic construction and phraseology.

PAGE 9. l. 98. *weary tendrils,* tired with holding up the boughs, heavy with fruit.

l. 103. *Silenus,* the nurse and teacher of Bacchus—a demigod of the woods.

PAGE 10. l. 115. *Circean.* Circe was the great enchantress who turned the followers of Ulysses into swine. Cf. *Comus,* ll. 46–54, and *Odyssey,* x.

PAGE 11. l. 132. *swoon'd serpent.* Evidently, in the exercise of her magic, power had gone out of her.

l. 133. *lythe,* quick-acting.

Caducean charm. Caduceus was the name of Hermes' staff of wondrous powers, the touch of which, evidently, was powerful to give the serpent human form.

l. 136. *like a moon in wane.* Cf. the picture of Cynthia, *Endymion,* iii. 72 sq.

l. 138. *like a flower . . . hour.* Perhaps a reminiscence of Milton's ' at shut of evening flowers.' *Paradise Lost,* ix. 278.

PAGE 12. l. 148. *besprent,* sprinkled.

l. 158. *brede,* embroidery. Cf. *Ode on a Grecian Urn.* v. 1.

PAGE 13. l. 178. *rack.* Cf. *The Tempest,* IV. i. 156, 'leave not a rack behind.' *Hyperion,* i. 302, note.

l. 180. This gives us a feeling of weakness and weariness as well as measuring the distance.

PAGE 14. l. 184. Cf. Wordsworth :

And then my heart with pleasure fills
And dances with the daffodils.

ll. 191–200. Cf. *Ode on Melancholy,* where Keats tells us that melancholy lives with Beauty, joy, pleasure, and

delight.   Lamia can separate the elements and give beauty
and pleasure unalloyed.

l. 195. *Intrigue with the specious chaos*, enter on an
understanding with the fair-looking confusion of joy and
pain.

l. 198. *unshent*, unreproached.

PAGE 15.   l. 207. *Nereids*, sea-nymphs.

l. 208. *Thetis*, one of the sea deities.

l. 210. *glutinous*, referring to the sticky substance which
oozes from the pine-trunk.   Cf. *Comus*, l. 917, ' smeared
with gums of glutinous heat.'

l. 211. Cf. l. 63, note.

l. 212. *Mulciber*, Vulcan, the smith of the Gods.   His
fall from Heaven is described by Milton, *Paradise Lost*,
i. 739–42.

  piazzian, forming covered walks supported by pillars,
a word coined by Keats.

PAGE 16.   l. 236. *In the calm'd . . . shades.*   In con-
sideration of Plato's mystic and imaginative philosophy.

PAGE 17.   l. 248. Refers to the story of Orpheus'
attempt to rescue his wife Eurydice from Hades.   With
his exquisite music he charmed Cerberus, the fierce dog
who guarded hell-gates, into submission, and won Pluto's
consent that he should lead Eurydice back to the upper
world on one condition—that he would not look back to
see that she was following.   When he was almost at the
gates, love and curiosity overpowered him, and he looked
back—to see Eurydice fall back into Hades whence he
now might never win her.

PAGE 18.   l. 262. *thy far wishes*, your wishes when you
are far off.

l. 265. *Pleiad.* The Pleiades are seven stars making a constellation. Cf. Walt Whitman, ' On the beach at night.'

ll. 266–7. *keep in tune Thy spheres.* Refers to the music which the heavenly bodies were supposed to make as they moved round the earth. Cf. *Merchant of Venice,* v. i. 60.

PAGE 20. l. 294. *new lips.* Cf. l. 191.

l. 297. *Into another,* i. e. into the trance of passion from which he only wakes to die.

PAGE 21. l. 320. *Adonian feast.* Adonis was a beautiful youth beloved of Venus. He was killed by a wild boar when hunting, and Venus then had him borne to Elysium, where he sleeps pillowed on flowers. Cf. *Endymion,* ii. 387.

Page 22. l. 329. *Peris,* in Persian story fairies, descended from the fallen angels.

ll. 330–2. The vulgarity of these lines we may attribute partly to the influence of Leigh Hunt, who himself wrote of

The two divinest things the world has got—
A lovely woman and a rural spot.

It was an influence which Keats, with the development of his own character and genius, was rapidly outgrowing.

l. 333. *Pyrrha's pebbles.* There is a legend that, after the flood, Deucalion and Pyrrha cast stones behind them which became men, thus re-peopling the world.

PAGE 23. ll. 350–4. Keats brings the very atmosphere of a dream about us in these lines, and makes us hear the murmur of the city as something remote from the chief actors.

l. 352. *lewd,* ignorant. The original meaning of the word which came later to mean dissolute.

PAGE 24. l. 360. *corniced shade.* Cf. *Eve of St. Agnes,* ix, ' Buttress'd from moonlight.'

ll. 363–77. Note the feeling of fate in the first appearance of Apollonius.

PAGE 25. l. 377. *dreams.* Lycius is conscious that it is an illusion even whilst he yields himself up to it.

l. 386. *Aeolian.* Aeolus was the god of the winds.

PAGE 26. l. 394. *flitter-winged.* Imagining the poem winging its way along like a bird. *Flitter,* cf. flittermouse = bat.

PART II.

PAGE 27. ll. 1–9. Again a passage unworthy of Keats's genius. Perhaps the attempt to be light, like his seventeenth-century model, Dryden, led him for the moment to adopt something of the cynicism of that age about love.

ll. 7–9. i. e. If Lycius had lived longer his experience might have either contradicted or corroborated this saying.

PAGE 28. l. 27. *Deafening,* in the unusual sense of making inaudible.

ll. 27–8. *came a thrill Of trumpets.* From the first moment that the outside world makes its claim felt there is no happiness for the man who, like Lycius, is living a life of selfish pleasure.

PAGE 29. l. 39. *passing bell.* Either the bell rung for a condemned man the night before his execution, or the bell rung when a man was dying that men might pray for the departing soul.

PAGE 31. ll. 72–4. *Besides . . . new.* An indication of the selfish nature of Lycius's love.

l. 80. *serpent.* See how skilfully this allusion is introduced and our attention called to it by his very denial that
it applies to Lamia.

Page 32. l. 97. *I neglect the holy rite.* It is her duty
to burn incense and tend the sepulchres of her dead kindred.

Page 33. l. 107. *blushing.* We see in the glow of the
sunset a reflection of the blush of the bride.

Page 34. ll. 122–3. *sole perhaps . . . roof.* Notice that
Keats only says 'perhaps', but it gives a trembling
unreality at once to the magic palace. Cf. Coleridge's
Kubla Khan :

> With music loud and long
> I would build that dome in air.

Page 36. l. 155. *demesne,* dwelling. More commonly
a domain. *Hyperion,* i. 298. *Sonnet*—'On first looking
into Chapman's Homer.'

Page 38. l. 187. *Ceres' horn.* Ceres was the goddess
of harvest, the mother of Proserpine (*Lamia,* i. 63, note).
Her horn is filled with the fruits of the earth, and is
symbolic of plenty.

Page 39. l. 200. *vowel'd undersong,* in contrast to the
harsh, guttural and consonantal sound of Teutonic
languages.

Page 40. l. 213. *meridian,* mid-day. Bacchus was
supreme, as is the sun at mid-day.

ll. 215–29. Cf. *The Winter's Tale,* iv. iv. 73, &c., where
Perdita gives to each guest suitable flowers. Cf. also
Ophelia's flowers, *Hamlet,* iv. v. 175, &c.

l. 217. *osier'd gold.* The gold was woven into baskets,
as though it were osiers.

l. 224. *willow,* the weeping willow, so-called because

P

its branches with their long leaves droop to the ground, like dropping tears. It has always been sacred to deserted or unhappy lovers. Cf. *Othello*, IV. iii. 24 seq.

adder's tongue. For was she not a serpent ?

l. 226. *thyrsus.* A rod wreathed with ivy and crowned with a fir-cone, used by Bacchus and his followers.

l. 228. *spear-grass . . . thistle.* Because of what he is about to do.

PAGE 41. ll. 229–38. Not to be taken as a serious expression of Keats's view of life. Rather he is looking at it, at this moment, through the eyes of the chief actors in his drama, and feeling with them.

PAGE 43. l. 263. Notice the horror of the deadly hush and the sudden fading of the flowers.

l. 266. *step by step*, prepares us for the thought of the silence as a *horrid presence*.

ll. 274–5. *to illume the deep-recessed vision.* We at once see her dull and sunken eyes.

PAGE 45. l. 301. *perceant*, piercing—a Spenserian word.

INTRODUCTION TO ISABELLA AND THE EVE OF ST. AGNES.

In *Lamia* and *Hyperion*, as in *Endymion*, we find Keats inspired by classic story, though the inspiration in each case came to him through Elizabethan writers. Here, on the other hand, mediaeval legend is his inspiration ; the ' faery broods ' have driven ' nymph and satyr from the prosperous woods '. Akin to the Greeks as he was in spirit, in his instinctive personification of the lovely manifestations of nature, his style and method were really more naturally suited to the portrayal of mediaeval scenes, where he found the richness and warmth of colour in which his soul delighted.

The story of *Isabella* he took from Boccaccio, an Italian writer of the fourteenth century, whose *Decameron*, a collection of one hundred stories, has been a store-house of plots for English writers. By Boccaccio the tale is very shortly and simply told, being evidently interesting to him mainly for its plot. Keats was attracted to it not so much by the action as by the passion involved, so that his enlargement of it means little elaboration of incident, but very much more dwelling on the psychological aspect. That is to say, he does not care so much what happens, as what the personages of the poem think and feel.

Thus we see that the main incident of the story, the murder of Lorenzo, is passed over in a line—'There was Lorenzo slain and buried in,' the next line, 'There, in that forest, did his great love cease,' bringing us back at once from the physical reality of the murder to the thought of his love, which is to Keats the central fact of the story.

In the delineation of Isabella, her first tender passion of love, her agony of apprehension giving way to dull despair, her sudden wakening to a brief period of frenzied action, described in stanzas of incomparable dramatic force, and the ' peace ' which followed when she

> Forgot the stars, the moon, the sun,
> And she forgot the blue above the trees,
> And she forgot the dells where waters run,
> And she forgot the chilly autumn breeze ;
> She had no knowledge when the day was done,
> And the new morn she saw not—

culminating in the piteous death ' too lone and incomplete '

—in the delineation of all this Keats shows supreme power and insight.

In the conception, too, of the tragic loneliness of Lorenzo's ghost we feel that nothing could be changed, added, or taken away.

Not quite equally happy are the descriptions of the cruel brothers, and of Lorenzo as the young lover. There is a tendency to exaggerate both their inhumanity and his gentleness, for purposes of contrast, which weakens where it would give strength.

The Eve of St. Agnes, founded on a popular mediaeval legend, not being a tragedy like *Isabella*, cannot be expected to rival it in depth and intensity; but in every other poetic quality it equals, where it does not surpass, the former poem.

To be specially noted is the skilful use which Keats here makes of contrast—between the cruel cold without and the warm love within; the palsied age of the Bedesman and Angela, and the eager youth of Porphyro and Madeline; the noise and revel and the hush of Madeline's bedroom, and, as Mr. Colvin has pointed out, in the moonlight which, chill and sepulchral when it strikes elsewhere, to Madeline is as a halo of glory, an angelic light.

A mysterious charm is given to the poem by the way in which Keats endows inanimate things with a sort of half-conscious life. The knights and ladies of stone arouse the bedesman's shuddering sympathy when he thinks of the cold they must be enduring; ' the carven angels ' ' *star'd* ' ' *eager-eyed* ' from the roof of the chapel, and the scutcheon in Madeline's window ' *blush'd* with blood of queens and kings '.

Keats's characteristic method of description—the way in which, by his masterly choice of significant detail, he gives us the whole feeling of the situation, is here seen in its perfection. In stanza I each line is a picture and each picture contributes to the whole effect of painful chill. The silence of the sheep, the old man's breath visible in the frosty air,—these are things which many people would not notice, but it is such little things that make the whole scene real to us.

There is another method of description, quite as beautiful in its way, which Coleridge adopted with magic effect in *Christabel*. This is to use the power of suggestion, to say very little, but that little of a kind to awaken the reader's imagination and make him complete the picture. For example, we are told of Christabel—

> Her gentle limbs did she undress
> And lay down in her loveliness.

Compare this with stanza xxvi of *The Eve of St. Agnes.*

That Keats was a master of both ways of obtaining a romantic effect is shown by his *La Belle Dame Sans Merci*, considered by some people his masterpiece, where the rich detail of *The Eve of St. Agnes* is replaced by reserve and suggestion.

As the poem was not included in the volume published in 1820, it is given here.

La Belle Dame Sans Merci.

> Oh what can ail thee Knight at arms
> Alone and palely loitering ?
> The sedge has withered from the Lake
> And no birds sing.

Oh what can ail thee Knight at arms
   So haggard, and so woe begone ?
The Squirrel's granary is full
   And the harvest's done.

I see a lily on thy brow
   With anguish moist and fever dew,
And on thy cheeks a fading rose
   Fast withereth too.

I met a Lady in the Meads
   Full beautiful, a faery's child,
Her hair was long, her foot was light
   And her eyes were wild.

I made a garland for her head,
   And bracelets too, and fragrant zone,
She look'd at me as she did love
   And made sweet moan.

I set her on my pacing steed,
   And nothing else saw all day long,
For sidelong would she bend and sing
   A Faery's song.

She found me roots of relish sweet,
   And honey wild and manna dew,
And sure in language strange she said
   I love thee true.

She took me to her elfin grot,
   And there she wept and sigh'd full sore,
And there I shut her wild, wild eyes
   With kisses four.

And there she lulled me asleep,
    And there I dream'd, Ah! Woe betide!
The latest dream I ever dreamt
    On the cold hill side.

I saw pale Kings, and Princes too,
    Pale warriors, death pale were they all;
They cried, La belle dame sans merci,
    Thee hath in thrall.

I saw their starv'd lips in the gloam
    With horrid warning gaped wide,
And I awoke, and found me here
    On the cold hill's side.

And this is why I sojourn here
    Alone and palely loitering;
Though the sedge is withered from the Lake
    And no birds sing. . . .

NOTES ON ISABELLA.

Metre. The *ottava rima* of the Italians, the natural out-come of Keats's turning to Italy for his story. This stanza had been used by Spenser and the Elizabethans, and recently by Hookham Frere in *The Monks and the Giants* and by Byron in *Don Juan.* Compare Keats's use of the form with that of either of his contemporaries, and notice how he avoids the epigrammatic close, telling in satire and mock-heroic, but inappropriate to a serious and romantic poem.

PAGE 49. l. 2. *palmer,* pilgrim. As the pilgrim seeks for a shrine where, through the patron saint, he may worship God, so Lorenzo needs a woman to worship, through whom he may worship Love.

PAGE 50. l. 21. *constant as her vespers*, as often as she said her evening-prayers.

PAGE 51. l. 34. *within . . . domain*, where it should, naturally, have been rosy.

PAGE 52. l. 46. *Fever'd . . . bride.* Made his sense of her worth more passionate.

ll. 51-2. *wed To every symbol.* Able to read every sign.

PAGE 53. l. 62. *fear*, make afraid. So used by Shakespeare : e.g. ' Fear boys with bugs,' *Taming of the Shrew*, I. ii. 211.

l. 64. *shrive*, confess. As the pilgrim cannot be at peace till he has confessed his sins and received absolution, so Lorenzo feels the necessity of confessing his love.

PAGE 54. ll. 81-2. *before the dusk . . . veil.* A vivid picture of the twilight time, after sunset, but before it is dark enough for the stars to shine brightly.

ll. 83-4. The repetition of the same words helps us to feel the unchanging nature of their devotion and joy in one another.

PAGE 55. l. 91. *in fee*, in payment for their trouble.

l. 95. *Theseus' spouse.* Ariadne, who was deserted by Theseus after having saved his life and left her home for him. *Odyssey*, xi. 321-5.

l. 99. *Dido.* Queen of Carthage, whom Aeneas, in his wanderings, wooed and would have married, but the Gods bade him leave her.

silent . . . undergrove. When Aeneas saw Dido in Hades, amongst those who had died for love, he spoke to her pityingly. But she answered him not a word, turning from him into the grove to Lychaeus, her former husband, who comforted her. Vergil, *Aeneid*, Bk. VI, l. 450 ff.

l. **103.** *almsmen*, receivers of alms, since they take honey from the flowers.

PAGE 56. l. **107.** *swelt*, faint. Cf. Chaucer, *Troilus and Cressida*, iii. 347.

l. **109.** *proud-quiver'd*, proudly girt with quivers of arrows.

l. **112.** *rich-ored driftings*. The sand of the river in which gold was to be found.

PAGE 57. l. **124.** *lazar*, leper, or any wretched beggar; from the parable of Dives and Lazarus.

stairs, steps on which they sat to beg.

l. **125.** *red-lin'd accounts*, vividly picturing their neat account-books, and at the same time, perhaps, suggesting the human blood for which their accumulation of wealth was responsible.

l. **130.** *gainful cowardice*. A telling expression for the dread of loss which haunts so many wealthy people.

l. **133.** *hawks . . . forests*. As a hawk pounces on its prey, so they fell on the trading-vessels which put into port.

ll. **133–4.** *the untired . . . lies*. They were always ready for any dishonourable transaction by which money might be made.

l. **134.** *ducats*. Italian pieces of money worth about 4s. 4d. Cf. Shylock, *Merchant of Venice*, II. vii. 15, 'My ducats.'

l. **135.** *Quick . . . away*. They would undertake to fleece unsuspecting strangers in their town.

PAGE 58. l. **137.** *ledger-men*. As if they only lived in their account-books. Cf. l. 142.

l. **140.** *Hot Egypt's pest*, the plague of Egypt.

ll. **145–52.** As in *Lycidas* Milton apologizes for the intro-duction of his attack on the Church, so Keats apologizes for the introduction of this outburst of indignation against cruel and dishonourable dealers, which he feels is unsuited to the tender and pitiful story.

l. 150. *ghittern*, an instrument like a guitar, strung with wire.

PAGE 59. ll. 153–60. Keats wants to make it clear that he is not trying to surpass Boccaccio, but to give him currency amongst English-speaking people.

l. 159. *stead thee*, do thee service.

l. 168. *olive-trees.* In which (through the oil they yield) a great part of the wealth of the Italians lies.

PAGE 60. l. 174. *Cut . . . bone.* This is not only a vivid way of describing the banishment of all their natural pity. It also, by the metaphor used, gives us a sort of premonitory shudder as at Lorenzo's death. Indeed, in that moment the murder is, to all intents and purposes, done. In stanza xxvii they are described as riding 'with their murder'd man '.

PAGE 61. ll. 187–8. *ere . . . eglantine.* The sun, drying up the dew drop by drop from the sweet-briar is pictured as passing beads along a string, as the Roman Catholics do when they say their prayers.

PAGE 62. l. 209. *their . . . man.* Cf. l. 174, note. Notice the extraordinary vividness of the picture here—the quiet rural scene and the intrusion of human passion with the reflection in the clear water of the pale murderers, sick with suspense, and the unsuspecting victim, full of glowing life.

l. 212. *bream,* a kind of fish found in lakes and deep water. Obviously Keats was not an angler.

freshets, little streams of fresh water.

PAGE 63. l. 217. Notice the reticence with which the mere fact of the murder is stated—no details given. Keats wants the prevailing feeling to be one of pity rather than of horror.

ll. 219-20. *Ah . . . loneliness.* We perpetually come upon this old belief—that the souls of the murdered cannot rest in peace. Cf. *Hamlet*, I. v. 8, &c.

l. 221. *break-covert . . . sin.* The blood-hounds employed for tracking down a murderer will find him under any concealment, and never rest till he is found. So restless is the soul of the victim.

l. 222. *They . . . water.* That water which had reflected the three faces as they went across.

tease, torment.

l. 223. *convulsed spur,* they spurred their horses violently and uncertainly, scarce knowing what they did.

l. 224. *Each richer . . . murderer.* This is what they have gained by their deed—the guilt of murder—that is all.

l. 229. *stifling :* partly literal, since the widow's weed is close-wrapping and voluminous—partly metaphorical, since the acceptance of fate stifles complaint.

l. 230. *accursed bands.* So long as a man hopes he is not free, but at the mercy of continual imaginings and fresh disappointments. When hope is laid aside, fear and disappointment go with it.

PAGE 64. l. 241. *Selfishness, Love's cousin.* For the two aspects of love, as a selfish and unselfish passion, see Blake's two poems, *Love seeketh only self to please,* and, *Love seeketh not itself to please.*

l. 242. *single breast,* one-thoughted, being full of love for Lorenzo.

PAGE 65. ll. 249 seq. Cf. Shelley's *Ode to the West Wind.*

l. 252. *roundelay,* a dance in a circle.

l. 259. *Striving . . . itself.* Her distrust of her brothers is shown in her effort not to betray her fears to them.

dungeon climes. Wherever it is, it is a prison which keeps him from her. Cf. *Hamlet*, II. ii. 250–4.

l. 262. *Hinnom's Vale,* the valley of Moloch's sacrifices, *Paradise Lost,* i. 392–405.

l. 264. *snowy shroud,* a truly prophetic dream.

PAGE 66. ll. 267 seq. These comparisons help us to realize her experience as sharp anguish, rousing her from the lethargy of despair, and endowing her for a brief space with almost supernatural energy and will-power.

PAGE 67. l. 286. *palsied Druid.* The Druids, or priests of ancient Britain, are always pictured as old men with long beards. The conception of such an old man, tremblingly trying to get music from a broken harp, adds to the pathos and mystery of the vision.

l. 288. *Like . . . among.* Take this line word by word, and see how many different ideas go to create the incomparably ghostly effect.

ll. 289 seq. Horror is skilfully kept from this picture and only tragedy left. The horror is for the eyes of his murderers, not for his love.

l. 292. *unthread . . . woof.* His narration and explanation of what has gone before is pictured as the disentangling of woven threads.

l. 293. *darken'd.* In many senses, since their crime was (1) concealed from Isabella, (2) darkly evil, (3) done in the darkness of the wood.

PAGE 68. ll. 305 seq. The whole sound of this stanza is that of a faint and far-away echo.

l. 308. *knelling.* Every sound is like a death-bell to him.

PAGE 69. l. 316. *That paleness.* Her paleness showing her great love for him ; and, moreover, indicating that they will soon be reunited.

l. 317. *bright abyss,* the bright hollow of heaven.

l. 322. *The atom ... turmoil.* Every one must know the sensation of looking into the darkness, straining one's eyes, until the darkness itself seems to be composed of moving atoms. The experience with which Keats, in the next lines, compares it, is, we are told, a common experience in the early stages of consumption.

PAGE 70. l. 334. *school'd my infancy.* She was as a child in her ignorance of evil, and he has taught her the hard lesson that our misery is not always due to the dealings of a blind fate, but sometimes to the deliberate crime and cruelty of those whom we have trusted.

l. 344. *forest-hearse.* To Isabella the whole forest is but the receptacle of her lover's corpse.

PAGE 71. l. 347. *champaign,* country. We can picture Isabel, as they ' creep' along, furtively glancing round, and then producing her knife with a smile so terrible that the old nurse can only fear that she is delirious, as her sudden vigour would also suggest.

PAGE 72. st. xlvi–xlviii. These are the stanzas of which Lamb says, ' there is nothing more awfully simple in diction, more nakedly grand and moving in sentiment, in Dante, in Chaucer, or in Spenser '—and again, after an appreciation of *Lamia,* whose fairy splendours are ' for younger impressibilities ', he reverts to them, saying :

'To *us* an ounce of feeling is worth a pound of fancy ; and therefore we recur again, with a warmer gratitude, to the story of Isabella and the pot of basil, and those never-cloying stanzas which we have cited, and which we think should disarm criticism, if it be not in its nature cruel ; if it would not deny to honey its sweetness, nor to roses redness, nor light to the stars in Heaven ; if it would not bay the moon out of the skies, rather than acknowledge she is fair.'—*The New Times*, July 19, 1826.

l. 361. *fresh-thrown mould*, a corroboration of her fears. Mr. Colvin has pointed out how the horror is throughout relieved by the beauty of the images called up by the similes, e.g. 'a crystal well,' 'a native lily of the dell.'

l. 370. *Her silk . . . phantasies*, i.e. which she had embroidered fancifully for him.

PAGE 73. l. 385. *wormy circumstance*, ghastly detail. Keats envies the un-self-conscious simplicity of the old ballad-writers in treating such a theme as this, and bids the reader turn to Boccaccio, whose description of the scene he cannot hope to rival. Boccaccio writes : 'Nor had she dug long before she found the body of her hapless lover, whereon as yet there was no trace of corruption or decay ; and thus she saw without any manner of doubt that her vision was true. And so, saddest of women, knowing that she might not bewail him there, she would gladly, if she could, have carried away the body and given it more honourable sepulture elsewhere ; but as she might not do so, she took a knife, and, as best she could, severed the head from the trunk, and wrapped it in a napkin and laid it in the lap of the maid ; and having covered the

rest of the corpse with earth, she left the spot, having been
seen by none, and went home.'

PAGE 74. l. 393. *Perséan sword*. The sword of sharpness given to Perseus by Hermes, with which he cut off the
head of the Gorgon Medusa, a monster with the head of
a woman, and snaky locks, the sight of whom turned
those who looked on her into stone. Perseus escaped by
looking only at her reflection in his shield.

l. 406. *chilly* : tears, not passionate, but of cold despair.

PAGE 75. l. 410. *pluck'd in Araby*. Cf. Lady Macbeth,
' All the perfumes of Arabia will not sweeten this little
hand,' *Macbeth*, v. ii. 55.

l. 412. *serpent-pipe*, twisted pipe.

l. 416. *Sweet Basil*, a fragrant aromatic plant.

ll. 417-20. The repetition makes us feel the monotony
of her days and nights of grief.

PAGE 76. l. 432. *leafits*, leaflets, little leaves. An old
botanical term, but obsolete in Keats's time. Coleridge
uses it in l. 65 of ' The Nightingale ' in *Lyrical Ballads*.
In later editions he altered it to ' leaflets '.

l. 436. *Lethean*, in Hades, the dark underworld of the
dead. Compare the conception of melancholy in the *Ode
on Melancholy*, where it is said to neighbour joy. Contrast
Stanza lxi.

l. 439. *cypress*, dark trees which in Italy are always
planted in cemeteries. They stand by Keats's own grave.

PAGE 77. l. 442. *Melpomene*, the Muse of tragedy.

l. 451. *Baälites of pelf*, worshippers of ill-gotten gains.

l. 453. *elf*, man. The word is used in this sense by
Spenser in *The Faerie Queene*.

PAGE 78. l. 467. *chapel-shrift*, confession. Cf. l. 64.

ll. 469–72. *And when . . . hair.* The pathos of this picture is intensified by its suggestions of the wife- and mother-hood which Isabel can now never know. Cf. st. xlvii, where the idea is still more beautifully suggested.

PAGE 79. l. 475. *vile . . . spot.* The one touch of descriptive horror—powerful in its reticence.

PAGE 80. l. 489. *on . . . things.* Her love and her hope is with the dead rather than with the living.

l. 492. *lorn voice.* Cf. st. xxxv. She is approaching her lover. Note that in each case the metaphor is of a stringed instrument.

l. 493. *Pilgrim in his wanderings.* Cf. st. i, ' a young palmer in Love's eye.'

l. 503. *burthen,* refrain. Cf. *Tempest,* i. ii. Ariel's songs.

NOTES ON THE EVE OF ST. AGNES.

See Introduction to *Isabella* and *The Eve of St. Agnes*, p. 212.

St. Agnes was a martyr of the Christian Church who was beheaded just outside Rome in 304 because she refused to marry a Pagan, holding herself to be a bride of Christ. She was only 13—so small and slender that the smallest fetters they could find slipped over her little wrists and fell to the ground. But they stripped, tortured, and killed her. A week after her death her parents dreamed that they saw her in glory with a white lamb, the sign of purity, beside her. Hence she is always pictured with lambs (as her name signifies), and to the place of her martyrdom two lambs are yearly taken on the anniversary and blessed. Then their wool is cut off and woven by the nuns into the archbishop's cloak, or pallium (see l. 70).

For the legend connected with the Eve of the Saint's anniversary, to which Keats refers, see st. vi.

Metre. That of the *Faerie Queene.*

PAGE 83. ll. 5-6. *told His rosary.* Cf. *Isabella*, ll. 87-8.

l. 8. *without a death.* The 'flight to heaven' obscures the simile of the incense, and his breath is thought of as a departing soul.

PAGE 84. l. 12. *meagre, barefoot, wan.* Such a compression of a description into three bare epithets is frequent in Keats's poetry. He shows his marvellous power in the unerring choice of adjective; and their enumeration in this way has, from its very simplicity, an extraordinary force.

l. 15. *purgatorial rails*, rails which enclose them in a place of torture.

l. 16. *dumb orat'ries.* The transference of the adjective from person to place helps to give us the mysterious sense of life in inanimate things. Cf. *Hyperion*, iii. 8; *Ode to a Nightingale*, l. 66.

l. 22. *already . . . rung.* He was dead to the world. But this hint should also prepare us for the conclusion of the poem.

PAGE 85. l. 31. *'gan to chide.* l. 32. *ready with their pride.* l. 34. *ever eager-eyed.* l. 36. *with hair . . . breasts.* As if trumpets, rooms, and carved angels were all alive. See Introduction, p. 212.

l. 37. *argent*, silver. They were all glittering with rich robes and arms.

PAGE 86. l. 56. *yearning . . . pain*, expressing all the exquisite beauty and pathos of the music; and moreover seeming to give it conscious life.

PAGE 87. l. 64. *danc'd*, conveying all her restlessness and impatience as well as the lightness of her step.

l. 70. *amort*, deadened, dull. Cf. *Taming of the Shrew*, iv. iii. 36, ' What sweeting ! all amort.'

l. 71. See note on St. Agnes, p. 224.

l. 77. *Buttress'd from moonlight.* A picture of the castle and of the night, as well as of Porphyro's position.

PAGE 88. ll. 82 seq. Compare the situation of these lovers with that of Romeo and Juliet.

l. 90. *beldame*, old woman. Shakespeare generally uses the word in an uncomplimentary sense—' hag '—but it is not so used here. The word is used by Spenser in its derivative sense, ' Fair lady,' *Faerie Queene*, ii. 43.

PAGE 89. l. 110. *Brushing . . . plume.* This line both adds to our picture of Porphyro and vividly brings before us the character of the place he was entering—unsuited to the splendid cavalier.

l. 113. *Pale, lattic'd, chill.* Cf. l. 12, note.

l. 115. *by the holy loom,* on which the nuns spin. See l. 71 and note on St. Agnes, p. 224.

PAGE 90. l. 120. *Thou must . . . sieve.* Supposed to be one of the commonest signs of supernatural power. Cf. *Macbeth*, i. iii. 8.

l. 133. *brook*, check. An incorrect use of the word, which really means *bear* or *permit*.

PAGE 92. ll. 155-6. *churchyard . . . toll.* Unconscious prophecy. Cf. *The Bedesman*, l. 22.

l. 168. *While . . . coverlet.* All the wonders of Madeline's imagination.

l. 171. *Since Merlin . . . debt.* Referring to the old legend that Merlin had for father an incubus or demon, and was himself a demon of evil, though his innate wickedness was driven out by baptism. Thus his ' debt ' to the demon was his existence, which he paid when Vivien compassed his destruction by means of a spell which he had taught her. Keats refers to the storm which is said to have raged that night, which Tennyson also describes in *Merlin and Vivien*. The source whence the story came to Keats has not been ascertained.

PAGE 93. l. 173. *cates*, provisions. Cf. *Taming of the Shrew*, II. i. 187 :—

> Kate of Kate Hall—my super-dainty Kate,
> For dainties are all cates.

We still use the verb 'to cater' as in l. 177.

l. 174. *tambour frame*, embroidery-frame.

l. 185. *espial*, spying. *Dim*, because it would be from a dark corner ; also the spy would be but dimly visible to her old eyes.

l. 187. *silken . . . chaste.* Cf. ll. 12, 113.

l. 188. *covert*, hiding. Cf. *Isabella*, l. 221.

PAGE 94. l. 198. *fray'd*, frightened.

l. 203. *No uttered . . . betide.* Another of the conditions of the vision was evidently silence.

PAGE 95. ll. 208 seq. Compare Coleridge's description of Christabel's room : *Christabel*, i. 175–83.

l. 218. *gules*, blood-red.

PAGE 96. l. 226. *Vespers.* Cf. *Isabella*, l. 21, ll. 226–34. See Introduction, p. 213.

l. 237. *poppied*, because of the sleep-giving property of the poppy-heads.

l. 241. *Clasp'd . . . pray.* The sacredness of her beauty is felt here.

missal, prayer-book.

PAGE 97. l. 247. *To wake . . . tenderness.* He waited

to hear, by the sound of her breathing, that she was asleep.

l. 250. *Noiseless . . . wilderness.* We picture a man creeping over a wide plain, fearing that any sound he makes will arouse some wild beast or other frightful thing.

l. 257. *Morphean.* Morpheus was the god of sleep.
amulet, charm.

l. 258. *boisterous . . . festive.* Cf. ll. 12, 112, 187.

l. 261. *and . . . gone.* The cadence of this line is peculiarly adapted to express a dying-away of sound.

PAGE 98. l. 266. *soother*, sweeter, more delightful. An incorrect use of the word. Sooth really means truth.

l. 267. *tinct*, flavoured ; usually applied to colour, not to taste.

l. 268. *argosy*, merchant-ship. Cf. *Merchant of Venice*, I. i. 9, ' Your argosies with portly sail.'

PAGE 99. l. 287. Before he desired a ' Morphean amulet'; now he wishes to release his lady's eyes from the charm of sleep.

l. 288. *woofed phantasies.* Fancies confused as woven threads. Cf. *Isabella*, l. 292.

l. 292. ' *La belle . . . mercy.*' This stirred Keats's imagination, and he produced the wonderful, mystic ballad of this title (see p. 213).

l. 296. *affrayed*, frightened. Cf. l. 198.

PAGE 100. ll. 298–9. Cf. Donne's poem, *The Dream* :—
My dream thou brokest not, but continued'st it.

l. 300. *painful change*, his paleness.

l. 311. *pallid, chill, and drear.* Cf. ll. 12, 112, 187, 258.

PAGE 101. l. 323. *Love's alarum*, warning them to speed away.

l. 325. *flaw,* gust of wind. Cf. *Coriolanus,* v. iii. 74 ; *Hamlet,* v. i. 239.

l. 333. *unpruned,* not trimmed.

PAGE 102. l. 343. *elfin-storm.* The beldame has suggested that he must be 'liege-lord of all the elves and fays'.

l. 351. *o'er . . . moors.* A happy suggestion of a warmer clime.

PAGE 103. l. 355. *darkling.* Cf. *King Lear,* I. iv. 237: 'So out went the candle and we were left darkling.' Cf. *Ode to a Nightingale,* l. 51.

l. 360. *And . . . floor.* There is the very sound of the wind in this line.

PAGE 104. ll. 375-8. *Angela . . . cold.* The death of these two leaves us with the thought of a young, bright world for the lovers to enjoy ; whilst at the same time it completes the contrast, which the first introduction of the old bedesman suggested, between the old, the poor, and the joyless, and the young, the rich, and the happy.

INTRODUCTION TO THE ODE TO A NIGHTINGALE, ODE ON A GRECIAN URN, ODE ON MELAN- CHOLY, AND TO AUTUMN.

These four odes, which were all written in 1819, the first three in the early months of that year, ought to be considered together, since the same strain of thought runs through them all and, taken all together, they seem to sum up Keats's philosophy.

In all of them the poet looks upon life as it is, and the eternal principle of beauty, in the first three seeing them in sharp contrast; in the last reconciling them, and leaving us content.

The first-written of the four, the *Ode to a Nightingale*, is the most passionately human and personal of them all. For Keats wrote it soon after the death of his brother Tom, whom he had loved devotedly and himself nursed to the end. He was feeling keenly the tragedy of a world 'where youth grows pale, and spectre-thin, and dies', and the song of the nightingale, heard in a friend's garden at Hampstead, made him long to escape with it from this world of realities and sorrows to the world of ideal beauty, which it seemed to him somehow to stand for and suggest. He did not think of the nightingale as an individual bird, but of its song, which had been beautiful for centuries and would continue to be beautiful long after his generation had passed away; and the thought of this undying loveliness he contrasted bitterly with our feverishly sad and short life. When, by the power of imagination, he had left the world behind him and was absorbed in the vision of beauty roused by the bird's song, he longed for death rather than a return to disillusionment.

So in the *Grecian Urn* he contrasts unsatisfying human life with art, which is everlastingly beautiful. The figures on the vase lack one thing only—reality,—whilst on the other hand they are happy in not being subject to trouble, change, or death. The thought is sad, yet Keats closes this ode triumphantly, not, as in *The Nightingale*, on a note of disappointment. The beauty of this Greek sculpture, truly felt, teaches us that beauty at any rate is real and lasting, and that utter belief in beauty is the one thing needful in life.

In the *Ode on Melancholy* Keats, in a more bitter mood, finds the presence, in a fleeting world, of eternal beauty the source of the deepest melancholy. To encourage your melancholy mood, he tells us, do not look on the things counted sad, but on the most beautiful, which are only quickly-fading manifestations of the everlasting principle of beauty. It is then, when a man most deeply loves the beautiful, when he uses his capacities of joy to the utmost, that the full bitterness of the contrast between the real and the ideal comes home to him and crushes him. If he did not feel so much he would not suffer so much; if he loved beauty less he would care less that he could not hold it long.

But in the ode *To Autumn* Keats attains to the serenity he has been seeking. In this unparalleled description of a richly beautiful autumn day he conveys to us all the peace and comfort which his spirit receives. He does not philosophize upon the spectacle or draw a moral from it, but he shows us how in nature beauty is ever present. To the momentary regret for spring he replies with praise of the present hour, concluding with an exquisite description of the sounds of autumn—its music, as beautiful as that of spring. Hitherto he has lamented the insecurity of a man's hold upon the beautiful, though he has never doubted the reality of beauty and the worth of its worship to man. Now, under the influence of nature, he intuitively knows that beauty once seen and grasped is man's possession for ever. He is in much the same position that Wordsworth was when he declared that

Nature never did betray

The heart that loved her; 'tis her privilege,

> Through all the years of this our life, to lead
> From joy to joy: for she can so inform
> The mind that is within us, so impress
> With quietness and beauty, and so feed
> With lofty thoughts, that neither evil tongues,
> Rash judgments, nor the sneers of selfish men,
> Nor greetings where no kindness is, nor all
> The dreary intercourse of daily life,
> Shall e'er prevail against us, or disturb
> Our cheerful faith, that all which we behold
> Is full of blessings.

This was not the last poem that Keats wrote, but it was the last which he wrote in the fulness of his powers. We can scarcely help wishing that, beautiful as were some of the productions of his last feverish year of life, this perfect ode, expressing so serene and untroubled a mood, might have been his last word to the world.

NOTES ON THE ODE TO A NIGHTINGALE.

In the early months of 1819 Keats was living with his friend Brown at Hampstead (Wentworth Place). In April a nightingale built her nest in the garden, and Brown writes: 'Keats felt a tranquil and continual joy in her song; and one morning he took his chair from the breakfast table to the grass-plot under a plum, where he sat for two or three hours. When he came into the house I perceived he had some scraps of paper in his hand, and these he was quietly thrusting behind the books. On inquiry, I found those scraps, four or five in number, contained his poetic feeling on the song of our nightingale. The writing was not well legible, and it was difficult to arrange the stanza on so many scraps. With his assistance I succeeded, and this was his *Ode to a Nightingale*.'

PAGE 107. l. 4. *Lethe.* Cf. *Lamia*, i. 81, note.

l. 7. *Dryad.* Cf. *Lamia*, i. 5, note.

PAGE 108. l. 13. *Flora*, the goddess of flowers.

l. 14. *sunburnt mirth.* An instance of Keats's power of concentration. The *people* are not mentioned at all, yet this phrase conjures up a picture of merry, laughing, sunburnt peasants, as surely as could a long and elaborate description.

l. 15. *the warm South.* As if the wine brought all this with it.

l. 16. *Hippocrene*, the spring of the Muses on Mount Helicon.

l. 23. *The weariness . . . fret.* Cf. ' The fretful stir unprofitable and the fever of the world ' in Wordsworth's *Tintern Abbey*, which Keats well knew.

PAGE 109. l. 26. *Where youth . . . dies.* See Introduction to the Odes, p. 230.

l. 29. *Beauty . . . eyes.* Cf. *Ode on Melancholy*, ' Beauty that must die.'

l. 32. *Not . . . pards.* Not wine, but poetry, shall give him release from the cares of this world. Keats is again obviously thinking of Titian's picture (Cf. *Lamia*, i. 58, note).

l. 40. Notice the balmy softness which is given to this line by the use of long vowels and liquid consonants.

PAGE 110. ll. 41 seq. The dark, warm, sweet atmosphere seems to enfold us. It would be hard to find a more fragrant passage.

l. 50. *The murmurous . . . eves.* We seem to hear them.
Tennyson, inspired by Keats, with more self-conscious art,
uses somewhat similar effects, e.g. :

> The moan of doves in immemorial elms,
> And murmuring of innumerable bees.
>
> *The Princess*, vii.

l. 51. *Darkling.* Cf. *The Eve of St. Agnes*, l. 355, note.

l. 61. *Thou . . . Bird.* Because, so far as we are con-
cerned, the nightingale we heard years ago is the same as
the one we hear to-night. The next lines make it clear
that this is what Keats means.

l. 64. *clown*, peasant.

l. 67. *alien corn.* Transference of the adjective from
person to surroundings. Cf. *Eve of St. Agnes*, l. 16;
Hyperion, iii. 9.

ll. 69-70. *magic . . . forlorn.* Perhaps inspired by a
picture of Claude's, ' The Enchanted Castle,' of which
Keats had written before in a poetical epistle to his friend
Reynolds—' The windows [look] as if latch'd by Fays and
Elves.'

PAGE 112. l. 72. *Toll.* To him it has a deeply melancholy sound, and it strikes the death-blow to his illusion.

l. 75. *plaintive.* It did not sound sad to Keats at first,
but as it dies away it takes colour from his own melancholy
and sounds pathetic to him. Cf. *Ode on Melancholy* : he
finds both bliss and pain in the contemplation of beauty.

ll. 76-8. *Past . . . glades.* The whole country speeds past
our eyes in these three lines.

NOTES ON THE ODE ON A GRECIAN URN.

This poem is not, apparently, inspired by any one actual vase, but by many Greek sculptures, some seen in the British Museum, some known only from engravings. Keats, in his imagination, combines them all into one work of supreme beauty.

Perhaps Keats had some recollection of Wordsworth's sonnet ' Upon the sight of a beautiful picture,' beginning ' Praised be the art.'

PAGE 113. l. 2. *foster-child.*   The child of its maker, but preserved and cared for by these foster-parents.

l. 7. *Tempe* was a famous glen in Thessaly.

Arcady. Arcadia, a very mountainous country, the centre of the Peloponnese, was the last stronghold of the aboriginal Greeks.   The people were largely shepherds and goatherds, and Pan was a local Arcadian god till the Persian wars (c. 400 B.C.).   In late Greek and in Roman pastoral poetry, as in modern literature, Arcadia is a sort of ideal land of poetic shepherds.

PAGE 114. ll. 17–18. *Bold . . . goal.*   The one thing denied to the figures—actual life.   But Keats quickly turns to their rich compensations.

PAGE 115. ll. 28–30. *All . . . tongue.*   Cf. Shelley's *To a Skylark* :

Thou lovest—but ne'er knew love's sad satiety.

ll. 31 seq. Keats is now looking at the other side of the urn.   This verse strongly recalls certain parts of the frieze of the Parthenon (British Museum).

PAGE 116. l. 41. *Attic,* Greek.

brede, embroidery.   Cf. *Lamia*, i. 159.   Here used of carving.

l. 44. *tease us out of thought.*   Make us think till thought is lost in mystery.

INTRODUCTION TO THE ODE TO PSYCHE.

In one of his long journal-letters to his brother George, Keats writes, at the beginning of May, 1819: 'The following poem—the last I have written—is the first and the only one with which I have taken even moderate pains. I have for the most part dashed off my lines in a hurry. This I have done leisurely—I think it reads the more richly for it, and will I hope encourage me to write other things in even a more peaceable and healthy spirit.   You must recollect that Psyche was not embodied as a goddess before the time of Apuleius the Platonist, who lived after the Augustan age, and consequently the goddess was never worshipped or sacrificed to with any of the ancient fervour, and perhaps never thought of in the old religion—I am more orthodox than to let a heathen goddess be so neglected.'   *The Ode to Psyche* follows.

The story of Psyche may be best told in the words of William Morris in the 'argument' to 'the story of Cupid and Psyche' in his *Earthly Paradise*:

'Psyche, a king's daughter, by her exceeding beauty caused the people to forget Venus; therefore the goddess would fain have destroyed her: nevertheless she became the bride of Love, yet in an unhappy moment lost him by her own fault, and wandering through the world suffered many evils at the hands of Venus, for whom she must

accomplish fearful tasks. But the gods and all nature
helped her, and in process of time she was re-united to
Love, forgiven by Venus, and made immortal by the Father
of gods and men.'

Psyche is supposed to symbolize the human soul made
immortal through love.

NOTES ON THE ODE TO PSYCHE.

PAGE 117. l. 2. *sweet . . . dear.* Cf. *Lycidas,* ' Bitter
constraint and sad occasion dear.'

l. 4. *soft-conched.* Metaphor of a sea-shell giving an
impression of exquisite colour and delicate form.

PAGE 118. l. 13. *'Mid . . . eyed.* Nature in its appeal
to every sense. In this line we have the essence of all that
makes the beauty of flowers satisfying and comforting.

l. 14. *Tyrian,* purple, from a certain dye made at Tyre.

l. 20. *aurorean.* Aurora is the goddess of dawn. Cf.
Hyperion, i. 181.

l. 25. *Olympus.* Cf. *Lamia,* i. 9, note.

hierarchy. The orders of gods, with Jupiter as head.

l. 26. *Phoebe,* or Diana, goddess of the moon.

l. 27. *Vesper,* the evening star.

PAGE 119. l. 34. *oracle,* a sacred place where the god
was supposed to answer questions of vital import asked
him by his worshippers.

l. 37. *fond believing,* foolishly credulous.

l. 41. *lucent fans,* luminous wings.

PAGE 120. l. 55. *fledge . . . steep.* Probably a recollection of what he had seen in the Lakes, for on June 29, 1818,
he writes to Tom from Keswick of a waterfall which ' oozes

out from a cleft in perpendicular Rocks, all fledged with Ash and other beautiful trees'.

l. 57. *Dryads*. Cf. *Lamia*, i. 5, note.

INTRODUCTION TO FANCY.

This poem, although so much lighter in spirit, bears a certain relation in thought to Keats's other odes. In the *Nightingale* the tragedy of this life made him long to escape, on the wings of imagination, to the ideal world of beauty symbolized by the song of the bird. Here finding all real things, even the most beautiful, pall upon him, he extols the fancy, which can escape from reality and is not tied by place or season in its search for new joys. This is, of course, only a passing mood, as the extempore character of the poetry indicates. We see more of settled conviction in the deeply-meditative *Ode to Autumn*, where he finds the ideal in the rich and ever-changing real.

This poem is written in the four-accent metre employed by Milton in *L'Allegro* and *Il Penseroso*, and we can often detect a similarity of cadence, and a resemblance in the scenes imagined.

NOTES ON FANCY.

PAGE 123. l. 16. *ingle*, chimney-nook.

PAGE 126. l. 81. *Ceres' daughter*, Proserpina. Cf. *Lamia*, i. 63, note.

l. 82. *God of torment*. Pluto, who presides over the torments of the souls in Hades.

PAGE 127. l. 85. *Hebe*, the cup-bearer of Jove.

l. 89. *And Jove grew languid*. Observe the fitting slowness of the first half of the line, and the sudden leap forward of the second.

NOTES ON ODE

[' BARDS OF PASSION AND OF MIRTH '].

PAGE 128. l. 1. *Bards,* poets and singers.

l. 8. *parle,* French *parler.* Cf. *Hamlet,* i. i. 62.

l. 12. *Dian's fawns.*   Diana was the goddess of hunting.

INTRODUCTION TO LINES ON THE MERMAID TAVERN.

The Mermaid Tavern was an old inn in Bread Street, Cheapside.   Tradition says that the literary club there was established by Sir Walter Raleigh in 1603.   In any case it was, in Shakespeare's time, frequented by the chief writers of the day, amongst them Ben Jonson, Beaumont, Fletcher, Selden, Carew, Donne, and Shakespeare himself. Beaumont, in a poetical epistle to Ben Jonson, writes:

What things have we seen
Done at the Mermaid ! heard words that have been
So nimble and so full of subtle flame,
As if that any one from whence they came
Had meant to put his whole wit in a jest,
And has resolved to live a fool the rest
Of his dull life.

NOTES ON LINES ON THE MERMAID TAVERN.

PAGE 131. l. 10. *bold Robin Hood.* Cf. *Robin Hood,* p. 133.

l. 12. *bowse,* drink.

PAGE 132. ll. 16–17. *an astrologer's ... story.* The astrologer would record, on parchment, what he had seen in the heavens.

l. 22. *The Mermaid . . . Zodiac.* The zodiac was
an imaginary belt across the heavens within which
the sun and planets were supposed to move. It was
divided into twelve parts corresponding to the twelve
months of the year, according to the position of the moon
when full. Each of these parts had a sign by which it was
known, and the sign of the tenth was a fish-tailed goat,
to which Keats refers as the Mermaid. The word *zodiac*
comes from the Greek ζῴδιον, meaning a little animal,
since originally all the signs were animals.

INTRODUCTION TO ROBIN HOOD.

Early in 1818 John Hamilton Reynolds, a friend of
Keats, sent him two sonnets which he had written 'On
Robin Hood'. Keats, in his letter of thanks, after giving
an appreciation of Reynolds's production, says: 'In
return for your Dish of Filberts, I have gathered a few
Catkins, 1 hope they'll look pretty.' Then follow these
lines, entitled, 'To J. H. R. in answer to his Robin Hood
sonnets.' At the end he writes: 'I hope you will like
them—they are at least written in the spirit of outlawry.'

Robin Hood, the outlaw, was a popular hero of the
Middle Ages. He was a great poacher of deer, brave,
chivalrous, generous, full of fun, and absolutely without
respect for law and order. He robbed the rich to give to
the poor, and waged ceaseless war against the wealthy
prelates of the church. Indeed, of his endless practical
jokes, the majority were played upon sheriffs and bishops.
He lived, with his 'merry men', in Sherwood Forest, where
a hollow tree, said to be his 'larder', is still shown.

Innumerable ballads telling of his exploits were composed, the first reference to which is in the second edition of Langland's *Piers Plowman*, c. 1377. Many of these ballads still survive, but in all these traditions it is quite impossible to disentangle fact from fiction.

NOTES ON ROBIN HOOD.

PAGE 133. l. 4. *pall.* Cf. *Isabella,* l. 268.

l. 9. *fleeces,* the leaves of the forest, cut from them by the wind as the wool is shorn from the sheep's back.

PAGE 134. l. 13. *ivory shrill,* the shrill sound of the ivory horn.

ll. 15–18. Keats imagines some man who has not heard the laugh hearing with bewilderment its echo in the depths of the forest.

l. 21. *seven stars,* Charles's Wain or the Big Bear.

l. 22. *polar ray,* the light of the Pole, or North, star.

l. 30. *pasture Trent,* the fields about the Trent, the river of Nottingham, which runs by Sherwood forest.

PAGE 135. l. 33. *morris.* A dance in costume which, in the Tudor period, formed a part of every village festivity. It was generally danced by five men and a boy in girl's dress, who represented Maid Marian. Later it came to be associated with the May games, and other characters of the Robin Hood epic were introduced. It was abolished, with other village gaieties, by the Puritans, and though at the Restoration it was revived it never regained its former importance.

l. 34. *Gamelyn.* The hero of a tale (*The Tale of Gamelyn*) attributed to Chaucer, and given in some MSS. as *The Cook's Tale* in *The Canterbury Tales.* The

1082.2   R

story of Orlando's ill-usage, prowess, and banishment, in *As You Like It*, Shakespeare derived from this source, and Keats is thinking of the merry life of the hero amongst the outlaws.

l. 36. '*grenè shawe*,' green wood.

PAGE 136. l. 53. *Lincoln green*. In the Middle Ages Lincoln was very famous for dyeing green cloth, and this green cloth was the characteristic garb of the forester and outlaw.

l. 62. *burden*. Cf. *Isabella*, l. 503.

NOTES ON 'TO AUTUMN'.

In a letter written to Reynolds from Winchester, in September, 1819, Keats says: 'How beautiful the season is now—How fine the air. A temperate sharpness about it. Really, without joking, chaste weather—Dian skies— I never liked stubble-fields so much as now—Aye better than the chilly green of the spring. Somehow, a stubble-field looks warm—in the same way that some pictures look warm. This struck me so much in my Sunday's walk that I composed upon it.' What he composed was the Ode *To Autumn*.

PAGE 137. ll. 1 seq. The extraordinary concentration and richness of this description reminds us of Keats's advice to Shelley—'Load every rift of your subject with ore.' The whole poem seems to be painted in tints of red, brown, and gold.

PAGE 138. ll. 12 seq. From the picture of an autumn day we proceed to the characteristic sights and occupations of autumn, personified in the spirit of the season.

l. 18. *swath*, the width of the sweep of the scythe.

ll. 23 seq. Now the sounds of autumn are added to complete the impression.

ll. 25-6. Compare letter quoted above.

PAGE 139. l. 28. *sallows*, trees or low shrubs of the willowy kind.

ll. 28-9. *borne . . . dies.* Notice how the cadence of the line fits the sense. It seems to rise and fall and rise and fall again.

NOTES ON ODE ON MELANCHOLY.

PAGE 140. l. 1. *Lethe.* See *Lamia*, i. 81, note.

l. 2. *Wolf's-bane*, aconite or hellebore—a poisonous plant.

l. 4. *nightshade*, a deadly poison.

ruby . . . Proserpine. Cf. Swinburne's *Garden of Proserpine.*

Proserpine. Cf. *Lamia*, i. 63, note.

l. 5. *yew-berries.* The yew, a dark funereal-looking tree, is constantly planted in churchyards.

l. 7. *your mournful Psyche.* See Introduction to the *Ode to Psyche*, p. 236.

PAGE 141. l. 12. *weeping cloud.* l. 14. *shroud.* Giving a touch of mystery and sadness to the otherwise light and tender picture.

l. 16. *on . . . sand-wave*, the iridescence sometimes seen on the ribbed sand left by the tide.

l. 21. *She*, i.e. Melancholy—now personified as a goddess. Compare this conception of melancholy with the passage in *Lamia*, i. 190-200. Cf. also Milton's personifications of Melancholy in *L'Allegro* and *Il Penseroso.*

PAGE 142. l. 30. *cloudy*, mysteriously concealed, seen of few.

INTRODUCTION TO HYPERION.

This poem deals with the overthrow of the primaeval order of Gods by Jupiter, son of Saturn the old king. There are many versions of the fable in Greek mythology, and there are many sources from which it may have come to Keats. At school he is said to have known the classical dictionary by heart, but his inspiration is more likely to have been due to his later reading of the Elizabethan poets, and their translations of classic story. One thing is certain, that he did not confine himself to any one authority, nor did he consider it necessary to be circumscribed by authorities at all. He used, rather than followed, the Greek fable, dealing freely with it and giving it his own interpretation.

The situation when the poem opens is as follows:— Saturn, king of the gods, has been driven from Olympus down into a deep dell, by his son Jupiter, who has seized and used his father's weapon, the thunderbolt. A similar fate has overtaken nearly all his brethren, who are called by Keats Titans and Giants indiscriminately, though in Greek mythology the two races are quite distinct. These Titans are the children of Tellus and Coelus, the earth and sky, thus representing, as it were, the first birth of form and personality from formless nature. Before the separation of earth and sky, Chaos, a confusion of the elements of all things, had reigned supreme. One only of the Titans, Hyperion the sun-god, still keeps his kingdom, and he is about to be superseded by young Apollo, the god of light and song.

In the second book we hear Oceanus and Clymene his daughter tell how both were defeated not by battle or violence, but by the irresistible beauty of their dispossessors ; and from this Oceanus deduces 'the eternal law, that first in beauty should be first in might'. He recalls the fact that Saturn himself was not the first ruler, but received his kingdom from his parents, the earth and sky, and he prophesies that progress will continue in the overthrow of Jove by a yet brighter and better order. Enceladus is, however, furious at what he considers a cowardly acceptance of their fate, and urges his brethren to resist.

In Book I we saw Hyperion, though still a god, distressed by portents, and now in Book III we see the rise to divinity of his successor, the young Apollo. The poem breaks off short at the moment of Apollo's metamorphosis, and how Keats intended to complete it we can never know.

It is certain that he originally meant to write an epic in ten books, and the publisher's remark [1] at the beginning of the 1820 volume would lead us to think that he was in the same mind when he wrote the poem. This statement, however, must be altogether discounted, as Keats, in his copy of the poems, crossed it right out and wrote above, 'I had no part in this ; I was ill at the time.'

[1] 'If any apology be thought necessary for the appearance of the unfinished poem of Hyperion, the publishers beg to state that they alone are responsible, as it was printed at their particular request, and contrary to the wish of the author. The poem was intended to have been of equal length with Endymion, but the reception given to that work discouraged the author from proceeding.'

Moreover, the last sentence (from ' but ' to ' proceeding ')
he bracketed, writing below, ' This is a lie.'

This, together with other evidence external and internal,
has led Dr. de Sélincourt to the conclusion that Keats
had modified his plan and, when he was writing the
poem, intended to conclude it in four books. Of the probable contents of the one-and-half unwritten books Mr. de
Sélincourt writes : ' I conceive that Apollo, now conscious of his divinity, would have gone to Olympus, heard
from the lips of Jove of his newly-acquired supremacy,
and been called upon by the rebel three to secure the
kingdom that awaited him. He would have gone forth
to meet Hyperion, who, struck by the power of supreme
beauty, would have found resistance impossible. Critics
have inclined to take for granted the supposition that
an actual battle was contemplated by Keats, but I do
not believe that such was, at least, his final intention.
In the first place, he had the example of Milton, whom
he was studying very closely, to warn him of its dangers ;
in the second, if Hyperion had been meant to fight he
would hardly be represented as already, before the battle,
shorn of much of his strength ; thus making the victory
of Apollo depend upon his enemy's unnatural weakness
and not upon his own strength. One may add that
a combat would have been completely alien to the whole
idea of the poem as Keats conceived it, and as, in fact,
it is universally interpreted from the speech of Oceanus
in the second book. The resistance of Enceladus and
the Giants, themselves rebels against an order already
established, would have been dealt with summarily, and
the poem would have closed with a description of the

new age which had been inaugurated by the triumph of the Olympians, and, in particular, of Apollo the god of light and song.'

The central idea, then, of the poem is that the new age triumphs over the old by virtue of its acknowledged superiority—that intellectual supremacy makes physical force feel its power and yield. Dignity and moral conquest lies, for the conquered, in the capacity to recognize the truth and look upon the inevitable undismayed.

Keats broke the poem off because it was too 'Miltonic', and it is easy to see what he meant. Not only does the treatment of the subject recall that of *Paradise Lost*, the council of the fallen gods bearing special resemblance to that of the fallen angels in Book II of Milton's epic, but in its style and syntax the influence of Milton is everywhere apparent. It is to be seen in the restraint and concentration of the language, which is in marked contrast to the wordiness of Keats's early work, as well as in the constant use of classical constructions,[1] Miltonic inversions[2] and repetitions,[3] and in occasional reminiscences of actual lines and phrases in *Paradise Lost*.[4]

[1] e.g. i. 56 Knows thee not, thus afflicted, for a god
    i. 206   save what solemn tubes
    .   .   .   .   gave
    ii. 70   that second war
    Not long delayed.

[2] e.g. ii. 8 torrents hoarse   32 covert drear   i. 265 season due   286 plumes immense

[3] e.g. i. 35 How beautiful . . . self   182 While sometimes . . . wondering men   ii. 116, 122 Such noise . . . pines.

[4] e.g. ii. 79 No shape distinguishable. Cf. *Paradise Lost*, ii. 667.

    i. 2 breath of morn. Cf. *Paradise Lost*, iv. 641.

In *Hyperion* we see, too, the influence of the study of Greek sculpture upon Keats's mind and art. This study had taught him that the highest beauty is not incompatible with definiteness of form and clearness of detail. To his romantic appreciation of mystery was now added an equal sense of the importance of simplicity, form, and proportion, these being, from its nature, inevitable characteristics of the art of sculpture. So we see that again and again the figures described in *Hyperion* are like great statues—clear-cut, massive, and motionless. Such are the pictures of Saturn and Thea in Book I, and of each of the group of Titans at the opening of Book II.

Striking too is Keats's very Greek identification of the gods with the powers of Nature which they represent. It is this attitude of mind which has led some people— Shelley and Landor among them—to declare Keats, in spite of his ignorance of the language, the most truly Greek of all English poets. Very beautiful instances of this are the sunset and sunrise in Book I, when the departure of the sun-god and his return to earth are so described that the pictures we see are of an evening and morning sky, an angry sunset, and a grey and misty dawn.

But neither Miltonic nor Greek is Keats's marvellous treatment of nature as he feels, and makes us feel, the magic of its mystery in such a picture as that of the

tall oaks
Branch-charmèd by the earnest stars,

or of the   dismal cirque
Of Druid stones, upon a forlorn moor,

When the chill rain begins at shut of eve,
  In dull November, and their chancel vault,
  The heaven itself, is blinded throughout night.
This Keats, and Keats alone, could do ; and his achieve-
ment is unique in throwing all the glamour of romance
over a fragment ' sublime as Aeschylus '.

NOTES ON HYPERION.

Book I.

Page 145. ll. 2–3. By thus giving us a vivid picture
of the changing day—at morning, noon, and night—
Keats makes us realize the terrible loneliness and gloom
of a place too deep to feel these changes.

l. 10. See how the sense is expressed in the cadence
of the line.

Page 146. l. 11. *voiceless*. As if it felt and knew,
and were deliberately silent.

ll. 13, 14. Influence of Greek sculpture. See Introduction, p. 248.

l. 18. *nerveless . . . dead*. Cf. *Eve of St. Agnes*, l. 12, note.

l. 19. *realmless eyes*. The tragedy of his fall is felt in
every feature.

ll. 20, 21. *Earth, His ancient mother*. Tellus. See
Introduction, p. 244.

Page 147. l. 27. *Amazon*. The Amazons were a war-
like race of women of whom many traditions exist. On
the frieze of the Mausoleum (British Museum) they are
seen warring with the Centaurs.

l. 30. *Ixion's wheel*. For insolence to Jove, Ixion was
tied to an ever-revolving wheel in Hell.

l. 31. *Memphian sphinx*. Memphis was a town in Egypt near to which the pyramids were built. A *sphinx* is a great stone image with human head and breast and the body of a lion.

PAGE 148. ll. 60-3. The thunderbolts, being Jove's own weapons, are unwilling to be used against their former master.

PAGE 149. l. 74. *branch-charmed . . . stars.* All the magic of the still night is here.

ll. 76-8. *Save . . . wave.* See how the gust of wind comes and goes in the rise and fall of these lines, which begin and end on the same sound.

PAGE 150. l. 86. See Introduction, p. 248.

l. 94. *aspen-malady*, trembling like the leaves of the aspen-poplar.

PAGE 151. ll. 98 seq. Cf. *King Lear.* Throughout the figure of Saturn—the old man robbed of his kingdom—reminds us of Lear, and sometimes we seem to detect actual reminiscences of Shakespeare's treatment. Cf. *Hyperion*, i. 98 ; and *King Lear*, I. iv. 248-52.

l. 102. *front*, forehead.

l. 105. *nervous*, used in its original sense of powerful, sinewy.

ll. 107 seq. In Saturn's reign was the Golden Age.

PAGE 152. l. 125. *of ripe progress*, near at hand.

l. 129. *metropolitan*, around the chief city.

l. 131. *strings in hollow shells.* The first stringed instruments were said to be made of tortoise-shells with strings stretched across.

PAGE 153. l. 145. *chaos.* The confusion of elements from which the world was created. See *Paradise Lost*, i. 891-919.

l. 147. *rebel three.* Jove, Neptune, and Pluto.

PAGE 154. l. 152. *covert.* Cf. *Isabella*, l. 221; *Eve of St. Agnes*, l. 188.

ll. 156-7. All the dignity and majesty of the goddess is in this comparison.

PAGE 155. l. 171. *gloom-bird*, the owl, whose cry is supposed to portend death. Cf. Milton's method of description, '*Not* that fair field,' &c. *Paradise Lost*, iv. 268.

l. 172. *familiar visiting*, ghostly apparition.

PAGE 157. ll. 205-8. Cf. the opening of the gates of heaven. *Paradise Lost*, vii. 205-7.

ll. 213 seq. See Introduction, p. 248.

PAGE 158. l. 228. *effigies*, visions.

l. 230. *O . . . pools.* A picture of inimitable chilly horror.

l. 238. *fanes.* Cf. Psyche, l. 50.

PAGE 159. l. 246. *Tellus . . . robes*, the earth mantled by the salt sea.

PAGE 160. ll. 274-7. *colure.* One of two great circles supposed to intersect at right angles at the poles. The *nadir* is the lowest point in the heavens and the *zenith* is the highest.

PAGE 161. ll. 279-80. *with labouring . . . centuries.* By studying the sky for many hundreds of years wise men found there signs and symbols which they read and interpreted.

PAGE 162. l. 298. *demesnes.* Cf. *Lamia*, ii. 155, note.

ll. 302-4. *all along . . . faint.* As in l. 286, the god and the sunrise are indistinguishable to Keats. We see them both, and both in one. See Introduction, p. 248.

l. 302. *rack*, a drifting mass of distant clouds. Cf. *Lamia*, i. 178, and *Tempest*, iv. i. 156.

PAGE 163. ll. 311–12. *the powers . . . creating.* Coelus and Terra (or Tellus), the sky and earth.

PAGE 164. l. 345. *Before . . . murmur.* Before the string is drawn tight to let the arrow fly.

PAGE 165. l. 349. *region-whisper*, whisper from the wide air.

BOOK II.

PAGE 167. l. 4. *Cybele*, the wife of Saturn.

PAGE 168. l. 17. *stubborn'd*, made strong, a characteristic coinage of Keats, after the Elizabethan manner; cf. *Romeo and Juliet*, iv. i. 16.

ll. 22 seq. Cf. i. 161.

l. 28. *gurge*, whirlpool.

PAGE 169. l. 35. *Of . . . moor*, suggested by Druid stones near Keswick.

l. 37. *chancel vault.* As if they stood in a great temple domed by the sky.

PAGE 171. l. 66. *Shadow'd*, literally and also metaphorically, in the darkness of his wrath.

l. 70. *that second war.* An indication that Keats did not intend to recount this 'second war'; it is not likely that he would have forestalled its chief incident.

l. 78. *Ops*, the same as Cybele.

l. 79. *No shape distinguishable.* Cf. *Paradise Lost*, ii. 666–8.

PAGE 172. l. 97. *mortal*, making him mortal.

l. 98. *A disanointing poison*, taking away his kingship and his godhead.

PAGE 173. ll. 116–17. *There is . . . voice.* Cf. i. 72–8.

The mysterious grandeur of the wind in the trees, whether in calm or storm.

PAGE 174. ll. 133–5. *that old . . . darkness.* Uranus was the same as Coelus, the god of the sky. The 'book' is the sky, from which ancient sages drew their lore. Cf. i. 277–80.

PAGE 175. l. 153. *palpable,* having material existence; literally, touchable.

PAGE 176. l. 159. *unseen parent dear.* Coelus, since the air is invisible.

l. 168. *no . . . grove.* 'Sophist and sage' suggests the philosophers of ancient Greece.

l. 170. *locks not oozy.* Cf. *Lycidas,* l. 175, 'oozy locks'. This use of the negative is a reminiscence of Milton.

ll. 171–2. *murmurs . . . sands.* In this description of the god's utterance is the whole spirit of the element which he personifies.

PAGE 177. ll. 182–7. Wise as Saturn was, the greatness of his power had prevented him from realizing that he was neither the beginning nor the end, but a link in the chain of progress.

PAGE 178. ll. 203–5. In their hour of downfall a new dominion is revealed to them—a dominion of the soul which rules so long as it is not afraid to see and know.

l. 207. *though once chiefs.* Though Chaos and Darkness once had the sovereignty. From Chaos and Darkness developed Heaven and Earth, and from them the Titans in all their glory and power. Now from them develops the new order of Gods, surpassing them in beauty as they surpassed their parents.

PAGE 180. ll. 228–9. The key of the whole situation.

ll. 237–41. No fight has taken place. The god has seen his doom and accepted the inevitable.

PAGE 181. l. 244. *poz'd*, settled, firm.

PAGE 183. l. 284. *Like . . . string.* In this expressive line we hear the quick patter of the beads. Clymene has had much the same experience as Oceanus, though she does not philosophize upon it. She has succumbed to the beauty of her successor.

PAGE 184. ll. 300–7. We feel the great elemental nature of the Titans in these powerful similes.

l. 310. *Giant-Gods*? In the edition of 1820 printed ' giant, Gods ? ' Mr. Forman suggested the above emendation, which has since been discovered to be the true MS. reading.

PAGE 185. l. 328. *purge the ether,* clear the air.

l. 331. As if Jove's appearance of strength were a deception, masking his real weakness.

PAGE 186. l. 339. Cf. i. 328–35, ii. 96.

ll. 346–56. As the silver wings of dawn preceded Hyperion's rising so now a silver light heralds his approach.

PAGE 187. l. 357. See how the light breaks in with this line.

l. 366. *and made it terrible.* There is no joy in the light which reveals such terrors.

PAGE 188. l. 374. *Memnon's image.* Memnon was a famous king of Egypt who was killed in the Trojan war. His people erected a wonderful statue to his memory, which uttered a melodious sound at dawn, when the sun fell on it. At sunset it uttered a sad sound.

l. 375. *dusking East.* Since the light fades first from the eastern sky.

Book III.

PAGE 191. l. 9. *bewildered shores.* The attribute of the wanderer transferred to the shore. Cf. *Nightingale,* ll. 14, 67.

l. 10. *Delphic.* At Delphi worship was given to Apollo, the inventor and god of music.

PAGE 192. l. 12. *Dorian.* There were several 'modes' in Greek music, of which the chief were Dorian, Phrygian, and Lydian. Each was supposed to possess certain definite ethical characteristics. Dorian music was martial and manly. Cf. *Paradise Lost,* i. 549-53.

l. 13. *Father of all verse.* Apollo, the god of light and song.

ll. 18-19. *Let the red . . . well.* Cf. *Nightingale,* st. 2.

l. 19. *faint-lipp'd.* Cf. ii. 270, 'mouthed shell.'

l. 23. *Cyclades.* Islands in the Aegean sea, so called because they surrounded Delos in a circle.

l. 24. *Delos,* the island where Apollo was born.

PAGE 193. l. 31. *mother fair,* Leto (Latona).

l. 32. *twin-sister,* Artemis (Diana).

l. 40. *murmurous . . . waves.* We hear their soft breaking.

PAGE 196. ll. 81-2. Cf. *Lamia,* i. 75.

l. 82. *Mnemosyne,* daughter of Coelus and Terra, and mother of the Muses. Her name signifies Memory.

l. 86. Cf. *Samson Agonistes,* ll. 80-2.

l. 87. Cf. *Merchant of Venice,* i. i. 1-7.

l. 92. *liegeless,* independent—acknowledging no allegiance.

l. 93. *aspirant,* ascending. The air will not bear him up.

PAGE 197. l. 98. *patient . . . moon.* Cf. i. 353, 'patient stars.' Their still, steady light.

256 NOTES ON HYPERION.

l. 113. So Apollo reaches his divinity—by knowledge which includes experience of human suffering—feeling 'the giant-agony of the world'.

PAGE 198. l. 114. *gray*, hoary with antiquity.

l. 128. *immortal death*. Cf. Swinburne's *Garden of Proserpine*, st. 7.

> Who gathers all things mortal
> With cold immortal hands.

PAGE 199. l. 136. Filled in, in pencil, in a transcript of *Hyperion* by Keats's friend Richard Woodhouse—

> Glory dawn'd, he was a god.

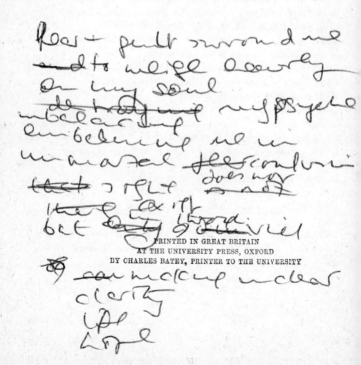

PRINTED IN GREAT BRITAIN
AT THE UNIVERSITY PRESS, OXFORD
BY CHARLES BATEY, PRINTER TO THE UNIVERSITY

Her gentleness was
beyond description

her ~~kind~~ love
~~extended to~~
had no limit
she gave her
soul to you
and wanted
nothing in return

~~Only~~.

Oh so sensitive ~~and~~

~~scared it was~~

so so sensitive
(that) she must
be treated with full
kindness
but this is not a loss
but a joy
a wonderful joy